AYO VAUGHAN-RICHARDS

Black & Beautiful

Collins

Published in association with
Johnson Products Co., Inc., Chicago
Cosmetologists to the Black
Race.

Acknowledgements

The Author and Publishers are grateful to the following for permission to reproduce photographs

All photographs by Juliet Highet except for,

Photos by permission of the author, p104 (bottom); 105; 106 (top right and bottom left); 126; 141; 144; 148.
Elegant Twins School of Hairdressing and Cosmetology p95 (bottom three); 99 (bottom right).
Photos of Coretta King and Winnie Mandela by permission of The Photo Source pp152–3.
Photos by kind permission of Jewel Lafontant and Eddah Gachukia p152 (top left and right).
Photos by kind permission of Johnson Products Co Inc., piv; 93 (bottom and top right); 95 (top two); 154.
Nigerian fabrics reproduced by kind permission of the National Council for Arts and Culture, Lagos.
Werner Forman Archive p5 (bottom).

Editorial consultant Juliet Highet
Illustrations by
Pinky Vaughan-Richards
Designed by
Sands · Straker Studios Limited

Printed in Italy by New Interlitho

Published by Collins, 8 Grafton Street, London W1X 3LA, United Kingdom.

10 9 8 7 6 5 4 3 2 1

Every effort has been made by the publishers to contact all the copyright owners but in some cases this has been impossible. It is hoped that any such omissions from this list will be excused.

First published 1986

ISBN 0 00 327807 7

APPRECIATION

This book gradually formed in my mind when, as Principal of the Lagos State School of Nursing, students and colleagues came to me with their problems, many of which concerned beauty and fashion. An insight into the very different problems of the manufacture and sale of cosmetics in developing countries came when I moved to the beauty business. A wide range of experience has been compressed within the covers of this book and the reader should appreciate the need to be selective in applying the contents to her own situation and be aware of the benefit of further personal research.

Firstly I must thank all those in the fields of nursing and also the beauty business. To them and the host of friends, many of them in the media, who gave so freely of their knowledge and advice and whose names do not appear below, I offer my sincere apologies, but it would require another book to list them all!

My special thanks go to Ayo Tella, Professor of Pharmacology at Lagos University and Chairman of the Lagos State Traditional Medicine Board, whose members enthusiastically gave me far more information on traditional cosmetics than could be fitted into this book. Dr Femi Vaughan advised me generally on health matters and Dr Maggie Ibru gave me invaluable guidance on our special skin, as well as on francophone African fashions.

Johnson Products of Nigeria taught me about the production and sales of cosmetics for Blacks. To Johnson Products of Chicago, 'the Cosmetologists to the Black Race', goes my profound gratitude for the sponsorship which enabled us to obtain the splendid colour photographs, most of which were taken by Juliet Highet who was also my long suffering editor.

Mrs Funke Akinyanju gave advice on Nigerian fashion houses. Elegant Twins School of Hairdressing and Cosmetology demonstrated hair styling, some of which is shown in the photographs. Judith Backary organised my portrait and many other West Indian friends provided information on the Caribbean. My thanks also go to the National Council for Arts and Culture, Lagos for information and photographs of Nigerian fabrics on page 122. My American cousins gave enthusiastic support which was echoed by a number of my Black sisters when we met at the End of Decade for Women's Conference in Kenya. The National Council of Women's Societies Nigeria also gave me great encouragement as well as useful hints.

My publishers, Kate Harris and Katie Mackenzie Stuart together with author and educationalist, Dr Elizabeth Pryse were my friends, philosophers, and guides who made my dream of a book on brains and beauty for Black women a reality. Abraham Akinbinu translated most of my scribble into immaculately typed pages in Lagos, while Carol Smith and Ruth Vaughan in Mallorca and London willingly abandoned other work to complete the outstanding chapters on time.

I thank my mother for teaching her daughters grace and elegance and my sons, Aruthur, who valiantly bashed out the first drafts on his student's typewriter, and Kenneth, for stoicly running errands. My daughter, Apinke was responsible for some of the illustrations and together with Betty provided a youthful viewpoint. My sisters Apinke and Taiwo and Chief Mrs Shodeinde made useful suggestions after reading the draft manuscript. Finally my husband gave me his time, full support and encouragement throughout my work which generated fresh strength in me, to carry on.

Ayo Vaughan Richards, Lagos, January 1986.

CONTENTS

Dedicated
to
My Daughters
Elizabeth Remi and Vanessa Apinke
Their Daughters
and
Their Daughters' Daughters

CHAPTER 1

A HEALTH AND BEAUTY BOOK WITH A DIFFERENCE

BLACK WOMAN

Naked woman, black woman
Clad in your colour that is life, in your form that is beauty!
I have grown up in your shade, the sweetness of your hands
    bound my eyes.
And now in the heart of summer and noon, I discover you,
    promised earth, from the tower of your sun-scorched
    neck
And your Beauty smites me to the full of my heart like the flash
    of an eagle.

Naked woman, dark woman!
Firm-fleshed ripe fruit, dark raptures of black wine, mouth
    making lyric my mouth
Savanna of sheer horizons, savanna quivering to the East wind's
    fervent caresses
Carved tom-tom snarling under the Victor's fingers
Your grave, contralto voice is the spiritual of the Beloved.

Naked woman, dark woman!
Oil sweet and smooth on the athlete's flanks,
On the flanks of the princes of Mali
Heaven-leashed gazelle, pearls are stars on the night of your
    skin
Delights of the spirit at play, red gold reflections on your
    shimmering skin.
In the shade of your hair, my anguish lightens with the nearing
    suns of your eyes.

Naked woman, black woman!
I sing your passing beauty, form that I fix in the eternal
Before jealous destiny burns you to ashes to nourish the roots
    of life.

by Leópold S. Senghor

The Arab influence.

A Mauritian woman, where Asians and Arabs have married Africans.

A West Indian woman.

A blend of American-Indian and Black American blood.

Daughter of a mixed marriage (between Nigerian and British parents.)

My sisters, we are Black, and it is our right to be beautiful. You and I have been endowed with our own individual and unique beauty and intelligence. It is our responsibility to enhance and build on those qualities which are available to us – charm, warmth, discipline, self-esteem, confidence, imagination, and above all a versatile mind in a strong and healthy body. These are what give us pride in being Black.

As you have picked up *Black and Beautiful,* you are already aware of this. Let us now explore together how you can best reach the goal of good health, and radiant beauty. This can be accentuated by the skilful use of creams, powders, lipsticks, fabulous hairstyles, and the latest fashions, but true beauty comes from the depths of our minds and reflects the state of our physical and mental health. Often it is not fully appreciated that this is the foundation upon which rests our success or failure in our efforts to look and feel good. Peace of mind is as important as the use of cosmetics. Self-knowledge and acceptance give you the freedom to flex your intellectual muscles as well as those of the body. Then you will achieve true beauty in which you will have inner harmony and happiness, with your body strong and fit, your movements, speech, actions and general aura, all radiating an admirable vitality and intelligence that draw people to you. You don't need to have perfect features ideally assembled – these are for cold marble statues. It may be a well-worn cliché, but real beauty radiates from within you.

OUR HERITAGE

Our journey begins with knowledge of ourselves and the world around us. As Blacks, we are one of the exquisite threads in the intricate fabric composed of the races of mankind. Every culture has its own explanation about the origin of man, many of which, across the world, are hearteningly parallel. According to the Yorubas of western Nigeria, God first sent a chicken and a dove to the earth with a snail shell full of earth, which they scattered with their feet into the marshes, thereby forming solid ground. God then created man at Ile-Ife, still the spiritual home of the Yoruba people. A convincing school of scientific thought agrees that mankind evolved in Africa, and then spread to the rest of the world.

Within Africa itself, there is a great variety of shades of colour, height, shape, face and body characteristics, ranging from the light-skinned peoples of the North to the darker ones south of the Sahara, but the great majority of all Africans are Negroes, one of the oldest races on the earth. The tiny Pygmies of present day Zaire adapted to the wetter rain forest conditions, and the statuesque Masai of Tanzania and Kenya to the drier regions. Mighty empires arose and fell in Africa, as they did elsewhere on the globe, but anthropologists and archaeologists leave us with no doubt that the continent was one of the cradles of civilisation. Everyone is aware of the splendours of the Nile Delta, but how many know of the impressive ruined courts and temples at Great Zimbabwe, staggering in their dimensions alone? Even up to the turn of the century, ethnocentric art experts could not accept that Africans had been responsible for the world-class art produced at the courts of Benin and Ife in Nigeria, or the Ashanti in Ghana.

Much to the surprise of the black Africans, pale-skinned strangers, the Portuguese, on their voyages of exploration, appeared along the coast at the end of the 15th century, and were recorded in the famous bronze reliefs of the time. The Benin Empire and Portugal regarded each other as equals, exchanging ambassadors. These Portuguese and other Europeans first came as traders and missionaries. Tragically, the slave trade followed, and millions of Africans were sold into slavery to be shipped to the American plantations, the West Indies and South America, losing not just their freedom, but also their cultural identities. During the 18th and 19th centuries, many Europeans emigrated to the Americas, which became a melting-pot of the races. 'Human races can all interbreed freely and they separate, mingle, and re-unite like the clouds do. Human races do not branch out like trees with branches that never come together', wrote H.G. Wells in his *Short History of the World*. The incredible range of skin-tone, hair-type and facial features in the contemporary Black woman reflects this heterogenous background and links those of us of African origin across the Black Diaspora.

Each of us is born with a unique set of genes passed on to us by our parents, which determine body type, sex, skin colour, physical growth and to a large extent, our personality and intelligence. After birth, we are physically and mentally moulded by the environment and culture in which we find ourselves, and every culture develops a social system to suit the environment from which it originates. Tradition is the means by which culture is handed down from generation to generation.

Africans are now taking more pride in their heritage, preserving that which is of value and discarding irrelevant imports. But when necessary we can still adopt or adapt virtues from other cultures. Mankind has progressed and created civilisations by combining the best from different groups, so that today for example, maths has been taken from the Arabs, science from the Greeks, some kinds of art from Africa and so on.

Ihase Anikulapo Kuti, one of the Queens of the famous Nigerian musician, who wear African cloth and make-up as a conscious political gesture of 'Blackism.'

A Ghanaian woman with her design interpretation of traditional African make-up.

CONCEPTS OF BEAUTY

'Beauty is in the eye of the beholder', and each society has evolved its own roles for women. Each too has its own concept of beauty. The attractive aspects of the shape and size of the female body for black societies are not the same as those for whites. For Africans, elaborate body decorations by painting, scarring or tattoing, intricately constructed hair-styles, curve-enhancing fashion created from hand-dyed or woven fabrics, set off by heavy hand-crafted jewellery, not only reflect an immensely rich cultural heritage, but also give an indication of values, beliefs and status. If a girl is given tribal markings or tatoos at an early age, she should be proud of them. They are African concepts of decoration, part of that deep Mother Earth syndrome, to which so many scattered black peoples ache to return. A modern African woman can enhance her beauty by using traditional products such as herbs and oils, augmented by modern cosmetics.

My sister, we have a rich and exciting heritage of being Black. Among the records of the past, we catch tantalising glimpses of great beauties like Nefertiti, Cleopatra and the Queen of Sheba. Since time immemorial, African beauty practices have influenced the world of cosmetics, and products like cocoa butter or the art of hair-plaiting are still doing so today. Famous white beauties (such as the French queen, Marie Antoinette) were reputed to have adapted African beauty formulas for their dressing tables.

Nefertiti

The legacy of slavery had long-term psychological implications. Until very recently, light skin colour was considered an economic and visual asset, usually accomplished by using bleaching creams which contain lead. As long ago as 1760, Lady Coventry died from the effects of regularly painting her face with white lead. Yet today, this poison is still an ingredient in most skin-lightening creams. In the last decade or so, the consciousness that 'Black is Beautiful' has not only helped us to feel 'Black and Proud', but also forced the Western world to re-define beauty. Pale skin is no longer a passport to social mobility and financial success. The growing pride we have in being Black should strengthen our resolve to improve our confidence and image. For this pride to be meaningful, we need to know more about our rich African cultural heritage.

The growing pride we have in being Black should strengthen our resolve to improve our confidence and image.

BEYOND BEAUTY

Today, as Black women, being 'Black and Beautiful' should no longer be our only aim in a world in which women have to continuously struggle for recognition and equal opportunities. The perception that women should have marriage, home-making and child-rearing as their only true vocation is diminishing. In any case, this concept is but a male-inspired illusion. Due to polygamy, some African women have needed to be financially independent of their husbands. Many entrepreneurial women on the west of the continent have over the centuries achieved considerable reputations as financial wizards. Some were called Cloth Queens, and travelled vast distances to enlarge their financial empires. To this day, examination of the small print of most contracts will show that it is African women who control the real wealth of the continent.

Black women are now in the position where they may take creative leadership of the world, and this should not only be in the areas of fashion and beauty, or in the classical fields of Black achievement – show business and sport. With discipline, self-esteem, self-knowledge, common sense in self-care, inner peace and development of intellect, we shall be robbed of nothing in life and can play our expected multiple roles in society. This requires a high degree of intelligence, sensitivity and confidence, without diminishing our unique feminine attributes. While we may enjoy feeling sexy and desirable and playing the games of beauty and fashion, what strong woman really needs to depend on her looks? The young urban African woman, removed from the rigorous morality of village life, does *not* need to sleep with her boss or college tutor to gain advancement in her career. Our efforts from now on must be directed forcefully towards looking for an extension of our horizons – towards the creation of a new dimension of Black achievement. You can make the start at any age and it is never too late to begin taking a really positive attitude toward improving your health, your image and your intellect.

My sister, why not start now?

CHAPTER 2

LET'S TALK ABOUT THE INNER YOU

In my introduction, I talked about Blacks generally, our origins, our culture and our natural heritage, with specific attention to the desirable beauty attributes and aspirations of Black women. Now let us talk about you.

Being liberated and beautiful means first discovering more about yourself, the Inner You. This chapter will suggest a method of undertaking a complete re-analysis of yourself and your image. In the face of rapid industrialisation and urbanisation, Black women living on the fast-changing African continent are now having to cope with stressful situations which are only too familiar to our sisters in the industrialised world. And increasingly, prolonged stress is being linked to health problems, both physical and mental.

We have to find and hold jobs and partners; and competition for these two scarce resources can be very fierce. We may have to cope with unwanted pregnancies, child delinquency, menopause and old age, without the support of the extended family – all set against a background of dangerous and invasive pollution, increasing violence, rape, drugs, social and environmental disintegration. Every generation has had its problems, and we shall overcome ours.

INNER QUALITIES

To be able to cope, we need to be strong, self-disciplined, self-confident, ready to accept responsibility and to question the effects of technology in our lives. We also need to ensure that we keep ourselves personally in peak condition. The quality of self-discipline is not as unpleasant as it may sound; it certainly pays immediate dividends in the ability to deal with the stresses of contemporary life. Problems there will always be, but how you face them is what counts. Even the adoption of a simple but effective beauty, exercise and relaxation routine will raise you in your own self-esteem. To thread your hair at night, thus preventing tangling; to exercise regularly even just three times a week; to remain aware of the beneficial or harmful nature of the substances we put inside our bodies – these factors are vital in maintaining physical health. But just as important is to put aside a quiet time for oneself, by oneself, every day – a gift to yourself alone. No woman is beautiful if she is evidently suffering from stress.

SELF-DISCIPLINE

Self-discipline in self-preservation extends from the simple but often demanding range of No's – to smoking, excessive alchohol and endless late nights, to the more subtle range of

Bringing up young girls with a sense of self-respect, dignity and fun. (She is wearing a wrapper and headtie of Aso oke hand-woven material from Nigeria.)

Yes's – the positive affirmation of belief in yourself. To maintain a high regard for your own ability to succeed in life is perhaps more of a challenge than 'giving up' this or that. No woman should ever say: 'I'm only a housewife'; 'I'm too young' or 'I'm too old.' Putting yourself down can cause as much damage to your health as drug-taking.

SELF-ESTEEM

Self-esteem comes from the proper evaluation of yourself as a person and belief in your own worth. If you are being influenced by traditional concepts of femininity that impose limitations on abilities, roles and functions, as happens in some parts of Africa, you are being brain-washed into inferiority. Don't believe it and don't accept it. Assert your God-given right to equality. Above all, don't belittle yourself. Learn to blow your own trumpet, for no one else will blow it for you. Every single avenue of self-expression is open to you, as a modern Black woman.

Self-esteem is central to all personal development and improvement and begins from childhood. By being loved and encouraged as a child, and being treated with respect, the small girl is given a high sense of her own worth. If someone is brought up in an environment in which she is constantly treated as if she were stupid or worthless, she grows up believing this and gradually forms more and more negative assumptions about herself, which become the yardstick by which she lives her life. A true evaluation will enable her to realise her real worth and with courage, develop the necessary belief in herself which can overcome this terrible handicap.

Being loved, accepted and appreciated are just as important in adulthood as in childhood. We all know the value of praise in our lives and in our work. Some people express only negative remarks about others, maybe out of jealousy or insecurity, and in this way destroy the self-confidence of those they continually criticise. Some women even react negatively to positive complimentary remarks about them. As an example, a woman who is being complimented about a lovely dress she is wearing, shrugs off the compliment by saying: 'Oh this old thing. I've had it for years.' By accepting such recognition gracefully, rather than rebuffing it, one increases one's own sense of well-being, and shows courtesy in return.

As far as beauty is concerned, nothing makes a woman more beautiful than the belief that she is beautiful. To be this confident, first, you have to accept that your general appearance, the way you look and feel and behave and the direction your life is taking, are entirely your responsiblity. You can't put the blame elsewhere or on anybody else. Put yourself firmly in control of your own life and don't be influenced too

much by other peoples' ideas. Treat all the beauty tips in magazines, the media and what is fashionable critically. Remember that their real motive is your money. You are the one to make the decision on the choices available for your beauty and health, using your common sense in making your selection.

Very few women will admit that they are totally satisfied with their health and looks. We would do well to pat ourselves on the back occasionally, avoiding too much self-criticism; Sophia Loren, surely one of the most beautiful film stars, relates in her lively book, *Women and Beauty,* that she wasn't always considered to be so. At thirteen, her nickname was 'Toothpick'. Even when she began her career in films, she was still not regarded as beautiful. Those were the days when all had to conform to an elusive standard of 'classical' beauty. Sophia's nose was deemed too long, her mouth too large, chin and lips too broad, hips too wide. And she was too tall! With self-esteem, hard work and above all, a structure to her life, Sophia Loren was able to transform herself not only into one of the world's most beautiful and ageless women, but also became a huge success, and not just in touting her good looks. As she points out, 'If a young woman is beautiful, but has no discipline, she will lose her looks as she grows older. If a plain woman is disciplined, she will become more beautiful with time.'

THE CHOICES YOU MAKE NOW

My sister, how do you set about your own self-improvement? Where and what you are now is the result of past choices that you have made. Where and what you will be in the future depend on the choices you make now.

MAKING TIME

What is stopping you? The obstructions to your progress are usually of your own making, for a woman's worst enemy in self-improvement is herself. First her in-built motherly instinct and altruistic nature, her urge to give unstintingly to her partner, her immediate family, and her extended family, often extend to neglecting herself and erasing her own identity. Secondly, many women feel unbearably busy, too weighed down by pressures of work and family, to find time to take stock of themselves and their image in the world. But in fact the only time when a woman may really be too occupied to look after herself properly, is when she has a new baby. However, this is precisely the time when she needs to muster all the help she can get, delegating responsibility, so that not only can she feel free to luxuriate in the role of motherhood and enjoy her baby, but also regain her feeling of self-confidence as a sexually desirable woman.

YOU CAN AFFORD TO BE BEAUTIFUL

Another self-imposed obstacle is old-fashioned ideas and ingrained bad habits. One such negative concept may be that looking gorgeous requires a bulging wallet. But you don't need the very latest fashions and outrageously expensive cosmetics to look wonderful. Those women who can afford to spend time and money on repeated visits to health farms, hairdressers and beauty salons, look good because they feel pampered. But it is possible to achieve that state of mind on a moderate income, with wise budgeting, informed choices, and the knowledge that because you are Black, you are inherently beautiful.

Who is stopping you? Nobody! It is *your* body. *You* make the choices that influence your total well-being, so let no one stop you from improving yourself. Your partner will be pleased with the results and you will gain a happier home because you, the foundation upon which it rests, will be radiant and healthy. You will feel freer to share yourself and your energies with those around you. Stop building road blocks on your path.

ASSESSING YOURSELF

Start now with a thorough assessment of yourself. You are the one most intimately concerned and have the most opportunity to study your weak and strong points. You are therefore able to be more critical than any outside observer, no matter how close or helpful they may be. Choose a time when life is not too hectic and you are unlikely to be disturbed, so that you can concentrate. Shut yourself in your room armed with a pad, pen and a positive attitude. Keep a good sense of humour, so you don't feel depressed after your self-assessment. Dress as you normally would during the day, whether in traditional or Western style, using make-up, if you usually do.

First sit down comfortably, close your eyes and relax. Be oblivious to anything else around you and focus your thoughts on yourself until you are in what I will call 'your inner space'. Ask yourself a series of questions, starting with: 'Am I satisfied and happy with my life and the direction it is taking?' If you are, can you still improve yourself? If you are not, why not? Do you see yourself as an angry or anxious woman, drained of all optimism with stress written all over your face? What is bothering you? Then open your eyes and mentally note your answers. Think hard about what you don't like about your life-style, and how you can improve it. It is never too late to make a change of direction. Help is available from so many quarters, some spiritual, others more immediately practical.

Now let's concentrate on your beauty. Stand some distance

Dancing is a great way of exercising to keep healthy.

from the mirror and take a long hard look at yourself, and sum up your general appearance. Note your impressions. Don't worry too much about your imperfections, it is unrealistic to be obsessed with your major flaws, which in any case may be considered by others to be part of your charm. Slowly consider all aspects of your body in detail, from head to toes, listing as you go along all that you consider to be your good features and those that can be improved. Remember to like yourself and your body. Your own kind of beauty, unique to you in this universe, is a precious individual asset that we shall be enhancing. So don't be like the two women Dr Paul Tourmier describes in his book *A place for you.* '. . . . A pretty woman confides in me that her first act when she goes into a hotel bedroom is to turn all mirrors with their faces to the wall. Another tells me that she has never been able to look at herself naked without a feeling of shame. This body of mine, she adds, is my enemy.'

YOUR HEALTH

As a nurse, now involved in the beauty business, I believe strongly that a peaceful yet inquiring mind in a healthy body are the prerequisites for lasting true beauty. Just as we visit the hairdresser several times a year, it really is essential to have regular medical and dental examinations. Some of the horrific manifestations of cancer in various parts of the body are nowadays considered to be directly linked to the stress of our changing lives. So why not take the simple precaution of an annual Smear Test for cervical cancer, particularly if you are over 40? You can also check you own breasts for any lumps. A lump may be cancerous so if you detect one, report it to your doctor immediately.

A healthy person is not usually conscious of the normal functions of her body, until things start to go wrong. So how is your health? Do you suffer from indigestion, constipation, chronic aches and pains? Are you breathless after exertion? Are you the lucky type that dies happily every night and jumps out of bed every morning feeling fully refreshed, or do you suffer from sleeplessness and constantly feel tired and listless? If it is the latter, of course you can consult your doctor. But beware of the tranquilisers and sleeping pills he may well prescribe, as these will just mask deeper symptoms of 'ill-at-ease'. That very word implies a lack of ease in your mental attitudes. As adult aware women, we have to take responsibility for our own health, rather than be used as the dustbin, or indeed – guinea-pig – for an uncaring pharmaceutical industry.

If you are living in the tropics, malaria is often a cause of

a general feeling of ill health. If you travel to a temperate climate or to a non-malarial area and do not take your prophylatics, it can flare up and the local doctor may not be able to diagnose it in time. If you suspect potentially harmful side-effects from habitual use of chemical anti-malarial tablets, there is an effective Homeopathic alternative, as with most other medicines.

YOUR POSITIVE ATTRIBUTES

Your self-assessment is not over yet. Having been brutally frank about your appearance, I hope that as your own best friend, you did not fail to assess your good and strong points. If you ignored your positive attributes, sit down again and make a list of them, giving your self-esteem the boost it needs. Each time you assess yourself, you can decide on the next step on your road to achieving your goal, enjoying your life more fully, since this is the key to beauty. At the age of 82, Lotte Berk, a well known exercise expert said:– 'I refuse to be unhappy, to give in, to be ill. . . . I wake up every morning and say, now what's happening today? And I look for something that is good that's going to make me feel happy. If I wake up feeling low, I determine to find something however small that will turn the day into something better and make it all worthwhile.'

A dancer of the National
Troupe of the Ivory Coast.

WHAT DO YOU WANT TO ACHIEVE

Being realistic about your looks and your life is not selfishness nor self-centred vanity. It is reaching out for your full potential to please and make yourself happy, and therefore ultimately others. So, what do you want to achieve?

- *To simply look better than ever, by being slimmer, improving your skin, starting to wear make-up.*
- *To change your whole life style, including your dress-style, your work, your total image.*
- *To feel healthy and more active, by exercising, giving up smoking and drinking too much alchohol.*
- *To broaden your horizon by joining the local library, achieving new career goals by attending evening classes or going to university.*
- *To get a new lease of life, using past experiences, failures and successes to build a positive future, perhaps taking up prayer or studying meditation, to realise the bliss of true freedom in everyday life.*

All are good, powerful and valid reasons and together add up to a thoroughly optimistic view of life that will create the new you. But you must remember that although a lot of things can be done to change a woman, from having your hair relaxed to having a face lift, nothing can be done to change your basic structure nor change the real you. So, accept and love who you are, be curious, creative, play games, have hobbies, dance, sing – most of all – keep on learning. Your goal is to improve yourself totally by giving expression to your inner self, not relying solely on external scientific and cosmetic aids, modern or traditional. Beauty of the external body is ephemeral, whilst beauty of the soul is eternal!

A Black American actress meditating by a statue of Buddha.

CHAPTER 3

EAT, DRINK AND BE HEALTHY

Feeling well stems from a well-balanced, organically-based diet.

'Eat, drink and be merry!'

Excellent advice! Eating and drinking as well as being vital to our survival are usually sources of continually enjoyable experiences, regardless of age or sex. A stormy controversy in American newspapers seemed to show that women prefer a good meal and a cuddle to having sex! However that may be, as eating and drinking are so vital, like sex, they have become surrounded by religious and cultural restrictions. The reasons for many of these restrictions have become lost in time, but others are essential health precautions. Eating pork or shell fish, for instance, is very risky in hot climates. Even in temperate Britain, until refrigeration became common, they were not eaten unless there was an 'R' in the month, which is from September to April, the cold winter months. In hot weather, pork can be infested with worms which, if not killed by thorough cooking, can prove fatal. Shell fish go bad very quickly in the heat.

THE NEW TABOOS

Now in the industrialised countries a whole lot of new taboos have been introduced so that it seems everything enjoyable is illegal, immoral, or fattening! Food seems to have a significance beyond our simple nutritional needs. Health disorders connected with eating often stem from psychological problems, and women would appear to suffer most. The hang-up may be on the relatively simple level of over frequent trips to the kitchen to assuage the feeling that one is lacking in love, or the problem may have become so serious that we starve ourselves into Anorexia Nervosa, believing we are still plump and therefore ugly.

Diet is the lynch pin of our health and beauty. If you are feeling well you are probably eating a balanced diet. Healthy people are usually energetic, good-natured and mentally alert. They have a clear skin, shiny hair and a good appetite. Good health depends upon our eating the right kinds, right amounts and right combinations of food. If you are not feeling well be sure you are not suffering from any disease such as malaria and be sure you are getting enough sleep. If you still feel less than 'on top of the world' your diet may well need a change. Never underestimate the importance of diet. A good diet will do more for your looks than the most expensive cosmetics!

Most people, especially those in Third World countries, have a monotonous diet, based on starch, which is augmented from time to time by feasts that help to make good its deficiencies. Thus the feast for the wake of an important member of a family in which an animal is roasted, helps repair the ravages of worry, stress and labour involved with the deceased's illness. The celebration of the closing of a fulfilled life is one aspect of such funerals, but also the meat consumed, often a rare delicacy, contains vital proteins and other nutrients.

In the industrialised countries, multi-national companies make huge profits by producing an infinite range of food and drink, which they persuade the ordinary woman, who does the shopping for the household, to buy, by seductive advertising and attractive but expensive and useless packaging. Over-eating of these processed foods leads to unhealthy fat, which has encouraged other fast-growing industries to get rich by producing diet foods, laden with other chemicals.

CORRECTING YOUR EATING PATTERN

Most of us feel we would look better with the loss of a few pounds. We cannot afford to abuse our bodies, either by over-eating the 'wrong' foods, nor by starvation. Crash diets never work for longer than a few weeks, usually because we revert to our old eating habits. Balance in your diet is the key. Unprocessed 'whole' foods are the answer.

Correcting the eating pattern by cutting down on fried foods, the white flour and white sugar products; eating less fats and salt; giving up soft drinks, and processed foods – will help you get slimmer. You will certainly feel healthier.

Are you snacking between meals? If the craving for a little something is irresistible, go for fruit or a carrot. If you are longing for something sweet, try dates, oranges, slices of pineapple, raisins or dried apricots, all of which are rich in vitamins.

So having cut out or given up all those deliciously dangerous foods, what on earth are we left with? The six most important nutrients our bodies need are proteins, carbohydrates, fats, vitamins, minerals and water. These act and react on our bodies in very complicated and subtle ways. The balance of these vital elements is the key to feeling and looking great.

PROTEINS

Proteins provide the primary building and repairing tissues that enable us to grow and maintain our bodies. They are necessary for the making of haemoglobin within the red corpuscles of the blood and for forming anti-bodies to fight infection. They also help in the clotting of the blood. Sources include fresh

foods, particularly meat, poultry, fish, eggs, dairy products, nuts, whole grains and most beans and pulses.

Beans and pulses are an excellent protein source, available all over the world, and at reasonable prices. They have a low calorie content and the lowest fat content of any of the protein foods, if you are interested in slimming. They also contain a high roughage content, which is vital to prevent constipation. Junk foods clog your system, and it is essential to include roughage or fibre for the proper functioning of your body. Other valuable sources of roughage are fruit, vegetables, whole grains such as brown rice, and whole cereals like brown bread.

CARBOHYDRATES

Carbohydrates satisfy our hunger and supply the immediate energy for physical work. This energy is measured in the calories of which we hear so much in connection with slimming. We use about 75 calories an hour when at rest, and with heavy housework about 400.

There are three forms of carbohydrates:– sugar, starches and cellulose. Sugar and starch are converted to glucose to produce short-term energy, and any that is not used is stored as fat. The cellulose has no energy value, but again provides that crucial fibre necessary for regulating the bowels.

Carbohydrates are found in sugars, cereals, fruits and vegetables, particularly of the root variety. Potatoes, yams, sweet potatoes and most other vegetables should if possible be eaten with their skins on, since these are a valuable source of Vitamin C. (However always peel cassava because the skin contains poisonous prussic acid.) A serving of baked potatoes, scrubbed and with their 'jackets' on, is not only delicious, but has only 100 calories, whereas chips or French-fries are high in calorie content, since they have been fried. Mashing potatoes halves their mineral content and also destroys some vitamins.

In fact the preparation of vegetables is extremely important, since skinning, slicing, mashing and above all – over-cooking – destroy much of their nutritional value. If you must cut up fruit and vegetables, do so in large chunks. Don't leave sliced vegetables around long before cooking or eating. Raw is best. Try to have at least one meal a day which includes uncooked vegetables, even if it's just a carrot or some (whole) lettuce leaves.

- *Don't forget that vegetables must be thoroughly washed before cooking, particularly if you are eating them raw. However you must be sure the water you use to wash raw vegetables is safe. If you boil your drinking water use boiled water for washing vegetables. A small amount of a suitable disinfectant like Milton or permanganate of potash can be added to unboiled water for washing vegetables. Then rinse well.*

FATS

Fats provide a source of energy and heat. They also make available to the body tissues the calcium which is crucial for its growth and repair, as well as acting as carriers for vitamins. Excess of fats leads to indigestion and obesity, while insufficient can lead to vitamin deficiency and skin disorders.

There are two types of fats – the saturated ones which are normally solid at room temperature, like butter, cream and lard which come from animal sources, and coconut and palm kernel oils. Unsaturated and polyunsaturated fats like vegetable and fish oils, are liquid at room temperature. Too high an intake of saturated fats is dangerous, because they contain high levels of cholesterol, which is linked to heart disease and high blood pressure. (Eggs also contain a lot of cholesterol.) You can substitute some of the vegetable fats for animal ones, good ones being ground-nut oil or sesame oil, though if you have been advised to follow a low fat diet, watch out for the invisible fats in avocadoes, nuts, mackerel and salmon fish, pork and the fat contained within red meat. Cold-pressed unsaturated vegetable oils are the best, but don't cook with sunflower oil, because when it is heated, it is believed to be carcinogenic (cancer-producing). If the oils are not cold-pressed, much of their nutritional value has been removed.

Vitamin supplements during pregnancy are vital, and should be continued during breast-feeding.

VITAMINS

Vitamins were discovered at the beginning of this century and as their chemical structure was not then known, they were named after the letters of the alphabet. They cannot replace food, and the body cannot absorb them without food, as they all work together and if the body is deficient in one, it may also need others.

When our diet is deficient in essential vitamins, serious diseases result, such as scurvy, rickets, beriberi and pellagra. On a more everday basis, vitamins prevent infections and anaemia. However, there is no point in consuming quantities of vitamin pills if your basic diet is well-balanced and nutritious. It is possible to provide all our vitamin requirements by a sensible diet, but at times, it is advisable to take supplements of vitamins and minerals, such as during pregnancy, while breast-feeding, and also if you are a vegetarian.

Vitamins fall into two groups. Those soluble in fat (A, D, E, F and K) need fats and minerals to be properly absorbed and most can be stored in the body. The others are soluble in water (B and C in particular) and have to be replenished daily as any excess is passed out in the urine.

Vitamin A is essential for good eye sight and in the treatment of eye disorders. It gives protection from respiratory infections, shortens the duration of diseases and promotes the growth of strong bones. This valuable vitamin also helps keep the skin, teeth, gums and hair in good condition and fights skin diseases such as open ulcers, boils and acne, when applied externally. A deficiency can result in dryness and early ageing of the skin. Sources of Vitamin A are carrots, green leafy vegetables, corn on the cob, marrow, asparagus, sweet potatoes, prunes, apricots, liver and egg-yolk.

The Vitamin B Complex at present consists of thirteen separate vitamins, some disguised as other vitamins and others without an alphabetical or numerical name, which should all be taken in balanced amounts, to obtain the best results. Stress conditions require additional intake of this vitamin complex.

Vitamin B1 (Thiamine) aids digestion, especially of carbohydrates, promotes growth and keeps the nervous system, muscles and heart working properly. A deficiency results in fatigue, forgetfulness, nerve pain, numbness and tingling. Sources include *brown* rice, brazil nuts, whole grain flour, wheatgerm, molasses, peas and broad beans.

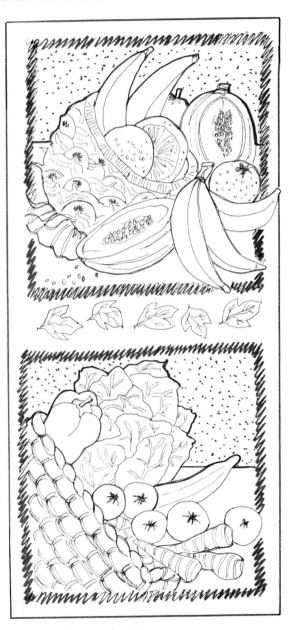

Vitamin B2 (Riboflavin, also known as Vitamin G) helps to break down all food, aids growth, reproduction and good vision. It promotes good skin, nails, hair and muscle tone. Deficiencies lead to bloodshot and itchy eyes, sensitive to bright lights. They also cause broken blood vessels, cracks and sores at the corners of the mouth, dermatitis, dandruff and split finger nails. Deficiencies are more likely for women on the Pill, and those pregnant or breast-feeding. These people should eat more liver, kidney, dark green vegetables like spinach, and also dairy products. It is also available in beans, avocadoes, and soya bean flour.

Vitamin B5 (Pantothenate Acid, Calcium Penthenate, Panthenol) is essential for the functioning of the adrenal gland, and necessary for the conversion of fat and sugar to energy. It helps in cell building, maintaining normal growth, and development of the central nervous system. It aids wound healing, fights infection and prevents fatigue. A deficiency results in irritability, headaches, blackouts, numbness, tingling muscles and cramps, and can lead to arthritis. Sources of B5 are whole grain products, fresh vegetables, yeast, liver, kidneys and eggs.

Vitamin B6 (Pyridoxine) is actually a group of substances that are closely related and act together. They aid digestion by the breakdown of foods and help form antibodies and red blood cells. They are also important in regulating the nervous system. A deficiency gives rise to irritability, nervousness, depression, mouth disorders, muscular weakness, anaemia and skin disorders. Women on the Pill may require to increase their intake. Vitamin B6 is found in most vegetables and meat.

Vitamin B12 (Cyanocobalamin, Cobalamin) is essential in the functioning of the body cells, especially those in the digestive and nervous systems and the bone marrow. It forms and regenerates blood cells, promotes growth and increases appetite in children. Deficiencies result in anaemia, unpleasant body odour and disturbances of the nervous system. Supplements may be helpful just before and during menstruation, and also for Vegans,

since its natural source occurs in meat and dairy products.

Biotin (Coenzyme R or Vitamin H) helps form fatty acids and then burns them together with carbohydrates for energy. Deficiences lead to fatigue, depression and to dermatitis. Sources are cauliflower, yeast extract, nuts, pulses, liver and kidneys.

Choline and Inositol are both members of the B complex family which aid the transmission of fats from the liver to the body cells and play a role in nerve transmission. A deficiency results in cirrhosis of the liver (also caused by alchohol

Peppers and tomatoes in a Lagos market contain Vitamin C.

abuse.) Stress and an excess of alchohol increases the need for an added intake of these vitamins, but do watch how easily an alchoholic habit can build up. With our contemporary life-styles and the fact that booze may always be around, it is so easy to have just one drink a day, which builds up into a real psychological and then physical dependancy.

Folic Acid (Vitamin M) is essential in the formation of blood cells and division of body cells, and aids in the digestion of protein. It is also needed for the utilisation of sugar and amino acids. Folic Acid improves lactation, promotes healthy skin and protects against internal food parasites and food-poisoning, and is therefore vital for breast-feeding mothers. A deficiency results in anaemia, low white blood count and depression. Drinkers should increase their intake of this vitamin.

Folic Acid is usually lost in cooking water, the prolonged heating of food or in canning processes, which is yet another reason to look at your cooking methods and choice of food. Canned foods are almost devoid of nutrition, and more expensive than fresh or frozen produce. If you boil your vegetables, do so extremely briefly in a small quantity of water, and don't throw away the liquid obtained. Use it for wonderful home-made vegetable or lentil soups – the ideal convenience food. If you heat food too long, it tastes ghastly anyway.

Vitamin C (Ascorbic Acid, Cevitamin Acid) plays an important part in the growth and repair of skin, ligaments, bones, teeth and gums. It is claimed to help to decrease blood cholesterol and many types of infection, including the common cold. A deficiency leads to a susceptibility to allergies, bad vision, tooth decay, bleeding gums and aching joints. Lack of Vitamin C, normally obtained from fresh fruit and vegetables, was responsible for the scurvy which was once common among sailors on long voyages.

The sunshine vitamin – D.

A snack of citrus fruit like oranges, instead of sugary products, helps combat allergies and fights tooth decay.

This vitamin is easily destroyed by heat or sunlight, and along with all the B vitamins, is soluble in water. Instead of boiling your vegetables, have you tried steaming, or stir-frying in a *tiny* bit of oil? Sources of Vitamin C are citrus fruits and cantaloupe melons, rose hips, green vegetables, guavas and tomatoes.

Vitamin D (Calciferol, Viosterol, Ergesterol) is essential for good bone and tooth structure. Deficiencies cause weak and brittle bones, spinal curvature, muscle cramp and joint pains, hardening of the arteries and rickets.

Vitamin D is known as the 'sunshine vitamin', as it can be produced by the body when the skin is exposed to sunlight and, in moderation, to ultraviolet light. Dark complexioned people living in far northern or southern climates, or those subject to smog, night workers or people whose clothing prevents sunlight from reaching the skin, such as nuns or women in purdah, may require supplementary boosts. Take some during the latter stages of pregnancy too, as the developing foetal bones need it.

Vitamin E (Tocopherol) unites with oxygen to protect the red blood cells and keep them from rupturing, and used externally, soothes and heals the skin. A deficiency may result in degeneration of reproductive tissues, sluggish circulation, varicose veins, muscle weakness and liver diseases. Sources are in pure vegetable oils, sunflower oil (used cold as a salad dressing for example), leafy vegetables and whole grains.

Vitamin K (Menadione) a complex of three vitamins formed by natural bacteria in the intestines. It prevents bleeding by stimulating the substances involved in clotting, and aids in the reduction of excessive menstrual flow. Natural sources are cauliflower, spinach, peas, cabbage and whole grains.

Vitamin supplements, in the form of tablets,

Calcium is essential for the building of bones and teeth.

capsules and liquids must always be kept in a cool, dark place. Get them from a chemist who also stores them properly, and check that their usage date has not expired. Even in the supposedly healthy world of vitamin supplements, there are products to be avoided. These are the synthetic vitamins, which in themselves contain harmful chemicals. Pay a little more and insist on the natural alternative. Vitamin supplements should be taken after meals, after your last meal of the day will be most effective.

MINERALS

Minerals, like vitamins, are essential elements of a healthy diet. They occur in minute quantities in the human body in highly concentrated form and are used in building and regulating it. They are essential for survival, so your daily intake is vital. There are about nineteen of them, contained in most natural foods.

Calcium is essential for the building of bones and teeth, for heart muscle regulation and for nerve transmission. A deficiency results in the deterioration of bones and teeth, muscle cramps and numbness in the limbs. While you are pregnant, don't forget to take extra calcium, as your baby is, in a sense, a parasite. The little darling will take all the calcium she needs for bone-building, leaving you bereft. The most immediate symptom of its deficiency will be your rapid tooth decay and muscular cramps. Calcium is found naturally in dairy foods, green vegetables and eggs.

Chlorine Sodium and (Sodium Chloride), better known as common salt, is perhaps the most indispensible mineral element for those of us living in hot climates, and was formerly one of the most important trade goods in Africa. It helps regulate the balance of acids and alkalis in the blood and is important for cellular activity. A deficiency results in nausea, vomitting, exhaustion, muscular cramps and respiratory distress.

In temperate climates, an excess of salt is dangerous, particularly to babies, whose

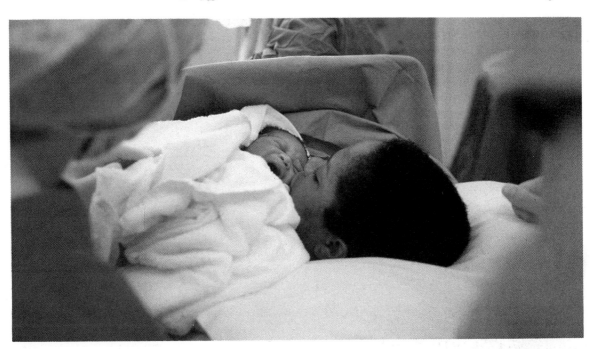

Take extra Calcium while pregnant, or the baby will take all yours!

kidneys can't excrete the excess. It is really not necessary to add salt to anybody's food in cooler temperatures, and our taste buds easily become addicted to this potentially dangerous substance. Beware of those processed foods with high salt concentrations such as crisps, tinned vegetables and salted meats. Do try to get the natural sea salt crystals, whose healthy properties have *not* been removed.

Copper is often associated with iron, helping in the production of red blood cells and hair pigment. It is needed for enzymes that build muscles and nerve fibres. A deficiency, which is rare, results in anaemia. A boost may however be necessary in pregnancy and during menstruation. You can try eating more fish, nuts, seeds, vegetables and prunes.

Iodine is necessary for the production of the thyroid hormone. Seafood and seaweed (of which the Japanese eat great quantities) are rich in iodine, for those living near the sea, but inland the source is plants. The amount found in plants will depend on how much they can extract from the soil. Deficiencies in the form of goitre, an abnormal swelling of the neck, is common in areas with soils poor in iodine. Other symptoms of deficiency are weight gain, nervous stress, drying of the skin and loss of hair.

Iron is most important as it is an essential constituent of haemoglobin, the red blood pigment responsible for the transportation of oxygen to the tissues. A deficiency results in anaemia, pallid skin, loss of energy, brittle nails and premature grey hair. Those who experience heavy menstrual bleeding should take an iron supplement at this time, but we should all eat fresh, raw vegetables at least once a day, for their natural iron content. Spinach and liver are excellent sources of iron. A cast-iron frying pan is an excellent cooking aid, and much healthier than an aluminium one.

Magnesium interacts with calcium, phosphorous and vitamins in the formation of bones and teeth, and the regulation of the function of muscles and nerves. Alchoholics and diabetics are often short of it. A deficiency results in muscular weakness, heart and circulatory

Zinc aids in digestion, helps in the formation of enzymes and proteins, and the elimination of carbon dioxide. Pregnant and older women and those on the Pill, may require a supplement. A deficiency causes enlargement of the prostrate gland, retarded growth and delayed maturity.

Zinc is removed from food by the process of refining, so this is yet one more vital reason to avoid refined (i.e. white) flour, rice, pasta and sugar. The refining process strips food of nutritional value, especially of the B group of vitamins. For instance, brown rice, pasta, sugar and whole wheat breads have 8 times the amount of Thiamine (Vitamin B1), 5 times the amount of Niacin and 3 times the amount of Riboflavin (Vitamin B2) than their white counterparts. What is even more serious, is that not content with removing essential vitamins and minerals, the manufacturers then put in harmful preservatives, additives and food colouring. And compare the taste of a chunk of whole wheat stone-ground granary bread or your local traditional whole grain bread with a pre-sliced sliver of white cardboard! Always study the labels on packets and cans to see just what it is you are putting into your system and that of your family.

Not all minerals are beneficial. Some are poisons, including lead, mercury and cadmium. The most common, lead, can be inhaled from traffic exhaust pollution, or ingested from the old-fashioned paints on some doors and windows, which children seem to love to pick at and swallow. Water from lead pipes is dangerous too.

WATER

Water is necessary to dissolve the foods that we eat and for the removal of waste. It cleanses the kidneys, eliminates toxins, regulates the body temperature, and lessens oily skin blemishes. It is our most important nutrient and half to three quarters of our weight is made up of it. A deficiency eventually leads to dehydration, with sunken eyes, a furred tongue and scanty urine.

Try to drink at least eight glasses of water a day, to flush out your system; the amount is

diseases, depression, dizziness, diarrhoea and a liability to convulsions. A high protein diet will supply sufficient magnesium for most needs.

Phosphorous is found in every cell of the body and is important for the growth and maintenance of cells. If you have sufficient protein and calcium in your diet, you will automatically be receiving enough phosphorous, as it is available in the same foods. However, older people do not absorb it well. A deficiency results in poor quality teeth and bones, stunted growth; cell regulation may also be disturbed.

Potassium, often in partnership with sodium, is necessary in muscle control, especially for the heart and in the stimulation of nerve impulses. It maintains the alkalinity of bile and blood. A deficiency, which is unlikely, except as a result of severe vomitting, diarrhoea or starvation, causes fatigue, muscular weakness, heart and respiratory disturbances. Natural sources are fish, potatoes, natural yoghurt and milk, meat, fruit and fruit juices.

obviously dependant upon the climate in which you live. If you drink a glass of warm water with a slice of lemon before bed, you will notice that your skin will soon become clearer.

A vast industry has grown up around bottled spring water; and of course this is very pure, but also very expensive to drink on a regular basis. If you are in any doubt about the purity of your tap-water, you can filter and then boil it for 5 minutes.

Besides water fresh fruit juices (diluted with water if necessary) can provide refreshing nutritious drinks.

FOOD AND THE FAMILY

Our tastes are formed at a very early age, and we tend to prefer the diet on which we were brought up. The reason why overweight parents tend to have obese children can be attributed to the whole family habitually eating lots of fattening foods, as much to inherited genes. Mothers often compete with each other to have the chubbiest baby, equating fat with health and beauty. But what they are really doing is sowing the seeds of an overweight problem in its adulthood. Children adore sweets, cakes and biscuits, which contain sugar, fats and processed flour, all of which are fattening, and tend to promote agression. They easily become addicted to sugar.

We tend to think of addiction in terms of drugs, alchohol and nicotine but sugar is among many everyday substances such as salt, coffee, tea and colas, which are also addictive. The withdrawal symptoms are not as terrible, but someone who suddenly stops her habitual cups of sweet coffee will crave for them and become irritable. Coffee and tea are stimulants, and if you are drinking more than a couple of cups a day, why don't you try lemon grass tea, grain-based or herbal alternatives, which are positively beneficial to your health? Hot peppers too are a stimulant, and potentially dangerous to those prone to stomach ulcers.

Alchohol can be very pleasant and provide you with a social boost but it is easy to destroy your physical and mental health by an excessive consumption. It is not for nothing that many

religions and philosophies forbid its use.

The changing diet of the industrialised nations is especially marked by the increased consumption of sugar among children and teenagers; and wealthy Third World countries, goaded on by aggressive advertising, seem eager to catch up. The result is an increase in dental decay and diabetes. Another decadent and highly questionable import is the mushrooming fast or junk food industry. Hamburgers, hot dogs, chips and similar foods manage to combine all that is worst for the diet – white bread, too much fat and preservatives! They are an additional temptation to the women who have rushed to work without any breakfast, and who have dull undemanding jobs. Frustrated women tend to nibble away continually at snacks, not realising how fattening this is, and also not as nutritious as a well-balanced meal.

Another problem that is being transferred to Third World countries is the use of chemical fertilisers and pesticides for crops, and the antibiotics injected into animals, particularly chickens. While it is not possible to do much about altering this on a personal basis, if you have a garden, you can follow 'Operation Feed Yourself', by growing your own organic vegetables and fruit. You can also elect to become a vegetarian, so that you will not be consuming meat, poultry or eggs crammed full of hormones and antibiotics. If you are a vegetarian, make sure that every element of your diet is of the maximum nutritional quality, so that you do not lose out, by denying yourself the instant protein of meat, fish and eggs. In the last decade or so, so many people in industrialised societies have revolted against the poisoning of our food that numerous alternative outlets for wholefood have sprung up. And even the supermarkets are taking note!

A healthy diet means avoiding some things but it also means eating a vast variety of delicious foods. So take heart; eat, drink and be healthy and beautiful.

We tend to prefer the diet on which we were brought up.

CHAPTER 4

EXERCISE IS FUN!

'That which is used develops, that which is not, wastes away' Hippocrates

In the last ten years exercise has become acceptable and even fashionable for women. It is every woman's right to feel fit, and although exercise alone will not make you slimmer, in combination with the nutritious diet we have described, you will look and feel a million dollars. You will feel well because regular training tones up muscles and firms up the flesh. You will look well because your body is working for you; you are not its prisoner. You will be making a positive contribution towards your own sense of well-being if your day includes sufficient exercise.

There are no special exercises for Black women. We need fitness, to feel our bodies are 'in tune' and yet capable of relaxation just as much as our sisters the world over. Many African women get enough exercise using a pestle and mortar to grind food, washing, cleaning and carrying out other household tasks. Even climbing up and down stairs and walking to the market probably give you more

exercise than you realise. If you have a maid don't leave everything to her, you need the exercise too!

I have a regime of simple exercises which are described at the end of this chapter. They are an aid to digestion and keep me fit and trim. They also prevent an old back injury from troubling me. Ideal exercise should be rhythmic and repetitive and use the large muscle groups of the body (especially those of the abdomen and pelvic areas) in smooth and continuous motions.

If you want to include some exercise in your daily routine, one of the best ways is to walk rather than take the car or bus. Walking is an excellent form of exercise in virtually every way. If you are reasonably fit you should be able to manage one mile in twenty minutes twice a day. This can be broken down into shorter periods as you go about your daily activities, travelling to work or to the market. Done regularly and briskly, conditioning can be achieved so that the body responds to physical demands without an excessive increase in the heart rate or blood pressure and without undue fatigue.

You may want to take up other forms of exercise. It is vital to proceed with common sense and caution. Exercise has become big business. Fortunes have been made from selling sportsclothes and equipment from building gyms and running clubs. Do not be beguiled into taking on more than you are able. Women in particular are prone to damage as they have lighter bone structure and more delicate ligaments and tendons than men. Women who exercise excessively and weigh very little may lose their menstrual cycles. When exercising, stop if you feel exhausted, especially if this is accompanied by nausea or dizziness. Rest, and resist any urging from others to carry on. We do not have to choose a form of exercise that brings us to this point. There are others that can give us equal satisfaction. Do not exercise if you are suffering from a viral infection as this can damage the heart although you may only find this out years later.

If you are out of shape, and have taken no physical exercise for years you must start gently, building up gradually. If you are over 35 or suffering from any kind of medical condition such as high blood pressure, heart disease, diabetes, or even if you are really overweight you should consult your doctor before starting. However do start; remember, following an exercise programme will be great fun.

CHOOSING YOUR EXERCISE!

Swimming is a splendid form of exercise. Aerobic dancing is good if you have the facilities. Cycling is fine in country areas but do be careful in heavy traffic. It may also be hard on the knees, especially for older people! Jogging has become very popular. If you are going to jog, start with just about ten minutes a day. Try and avoid the polluted city air. To jog peacefully along, maintaining a steady rhythm, smelling the flowers and enjoying the fresh morning air can be a really exhilarating experience.

Jogging for about half an hour each day will keep you trim and make you feel marvellous.

Hatha Yoga – the Plough posture.

Other forms of exercise from the East have evolved from methods of self-defence. They include Judo, Karate and Jujitsu. These develop balance, co-ordination, flexibility and mental concentration. If you can find classes in these sports they are worth learning. The knowledge that one can defend oneself if necessary gives a profound sense of self-confidence in an insecure world.

Dancing is a wonderful form of exercise. Disco, African, classical ballet, jazz tap and even belly dancing involve rhythmic repetitive movements. Whether you join a class or just dance at social events you will be doing your body a good turn!

Whatever form of exercise you have decided to follow, you can choose from a wide range of fashionable clothes to wear for it. However do bear safety and comfort in mind as well as your appearance. If you have selected jogging make sure that you have strong, flexible trainers with firm thick heels, since you may well have to jog over pavements and poor quality shoes may jar your heels and

Another non-competitive method of attaining physical fitness and a firm figure is by Yoga. Devised thousands of years ago in India, Yoga is a method of attaining 'total enlightenment'. As it is practised on a more physical level it is called 'Hatha Yoga' and involves various forms of stretching exercises. Yoga is the perfect form of exercise for you to do at home, requiring little space and no special equipment, but it is also an excellent idea to attend a class regularly to be sure you are following the system correctly. Everyone practising Yoga proceeds at her own pace, usually starting with warming up exercises and ending with a brief period of complete relaxation or meditation. These practices are wise before and after any form of exercise or sport. Before vigorous exercise bend and straighten, and shake your legs and arms a few times. After vigorous exertion slow down to a very slow walk, then lie down for a few minutes, flat on your back, acknowledge that deep feeling of relaxation and well-being. Do not take cold drinks immediately after exercising.

Dancercise your flab away!

Acceptance of sports and exercise has radically affected fashion during the last decade.

therefore your whole back. Select a stretchy yet supportive bra and loose tracksuit or T-shirt and shorts, made from natural fibres such as cotton, because you will sweat.

Make sure you are fit enough to enjoy your work and leisure. Women in control of their bodies are women in control of their lives. If you change your pattern of activities and give your muscles unaccustomed tasks they may show their displeasure at the extra exertion by giving you a display of aches and pains! But they should soon settle down to their new way of life, providing you are not overdoing things. If they do not, see a doctor. If once in a while you dance the night away, you may pay for your enjoyment with aches and pains in the morning. That's perfectly normal. It was worth it, wasn't it?

Regular exercise (whether you are incorporating it into your ordinary activities or whether you have decided to learn and follow a particular programme) increases and improves the capacity of your lungs. It strengthens the heart, tones up your muscles and ensures good circulation. Your skin will also benefit. Exercise will sharpen your intellect, give you confidence and help to protect you from stress and fatigue.

Standing correctly.

POSTURE

Exercise will help you look and feel good, but the way we stand, sit and move as we go about our every day business are also vital for our health and beauty.

A woman with poise is a woman with good posture. How you carry your body as you walk, sit, stand or bend, tells others about your personality, feelings, self-confidence and health. Remember that posture can make or mar your appearance, no matter how stunning or well-dressed you are.

'Bad' posture with slumped shoulders, and a protruding tummy, can affect your breathing, cause digestive problems and give you shoulder and back-ache.

STANDING

Stand before a full-length mirror, and study yourself carefully, assessing how you normally stand. Now try the 'correct' way. Place your weight evenly on both feet, keep your head up and back straight, your shoulders level and relaxed. Hold your tummy in, but don't be too tense. You should notice a marked difference, and yet feel comfortable and relaxed.

WALKING AND FEELING TEN FEET TALL

In cold climates people generally walk at a fast pace to keep warm. In hot climates, we tend to walk more slowly, for obvious reasons. Though you may be very hot, try not to walk so sluggishly, that you drag your feet on the ground. Apart from anything else, you will look depressed and 'down-at-heel.' Your shoes will tell you whether you have been balancing your weight on your feet correctly. If the soles and heels are worn down unevenly, or quickly wear out at the inner or outer edge, not only are you running up big bills at the shoe-menders, but you are also putting unnecessary strain on your body.

Even if you are not a fashion model on the catwalk, you can learn to walk gracefully. Practise by walking along an imaginary straight line in bare feet, or stretch out a thin strip of cloth or string about six feet long on the floor. Slowly walk down this, with your head erect and body held straight and balanced. Remember to drop those shoulders. Start off with your feet on either side of the line, but please don't look down until you finish, or you will ruin the whole effect! Your method of walking should feel erect and as relaxed and rhythmical as can be.

SITTING PRETTY

We often forget that sitting correctly is as important for our posture as it is for our health. If your life involves a lot of sitting and driving, make sure that your chair or car seat are comfortable, set at the right height and angle for you. Your seat should give you firm support in the hollow of your back, and not recline too much, so that your feet are off the ground. If your back is straight, you should automatically have a (relatively) flat tummy; but be aware that your weight should be supported, not by your thighs, but by the bones in your bottom. Naturally, keep your legs together, but if you cross them, do it either at the ankles, or more elegantly, by swinging one thigh right across the other, so that they are crossed high up. People in the public eye are taught to then align one leg with the other. But retain both positions only for relatively short periods, as otherwise you could develop unnecessary muscular tension or even aggravate varicose veins.

YOUR BACK

To lift anything from the floor or a low shelf, always bend at the knees, not at the waist. You will thus avoid one of the main causes of back problems.

Back trouble is an increasingly common complaint among Black women. If it is not due to medical or gynaecological conditions, it can be helped by specific exercises and correct posture. But please get professional advice and therapy in the case of serious back-ache. It can make your life a misery.

- *Never lift any heavy weights, if you can get help.*
- *If there's no one else around, or you are picking up a child, lift by bending at the knees, keeping your hands close to your body. Your stability is stronger and more balanced in this position.*
- *Beware of continually wearing high heels that throw you off balance, straining your lower back, especially if you are pregnant.*
- *Watch your weight, as an over weight condition can place unnecessary strain on your back muscles.*
- *When gardening or doing housework, don't overdo it, and stop when your back starts to hurt.*
- *Avoid a soft mattress or one that goes down in the middle, as it ruins the alignment of your body. If necessary, place a board under your mattress. Since you spend a third of your life asleep, purchase of a well-sprung mattress is one of your best investments. Otherwise, if money is a problem, you can place a thick sheet of foam on the floor, or on a bed with a solid base. Our rural sisters, some of whom sleep on mats on the floor, don't usually suffer from back-ache.*

FACIAL EXERCISE

Do not neglect your face in your exercise routine. Simple exercises can help to keep it firm and attractive.

Smiling is the best form of facial excercise especially as it indicates that you are feeling good. You can also do specific exercises by looking in the mirror and making funny faces at yourself. Not as daft as it sounds, since you will be twisting your face into such shapes and angles, that you'll probably burst out laughing anyway, a situation infinitely preferable to those tell-tale frown or worry lines.

Remember to moisturise your face and neck lavishly before starting, and repeat each exercise five times, but no more, or you will put into reverse gear all your good work.

- *Imagine you have smelt something really awful, so crunch your face up into your nose tightly, keeping your mouth shut. Relax.*
- *Open your mouth and eyes as wide as you can and stick your tongue right out. This strengthens your throat muscles.*
- *Fill your mouth with air, and with your fingers, tap your cheeks from the sides of your mouth to your ears, as you slowly let the air out.*
- *Make a big grin to stretch from ear to ear, tuck in your chin, pulling down your lower lip. This firms the frontal neck muscles.*
- *The best exercise to release face and neck tension is one you can do anywhere, for example, while sitting stationary in your car, or washing-up. Breathe in deeply, then very slowly rotate your head around and back, tilting it back slightly, in a complete circle. Repeat in the opposite direction. You don't have to do this many times before experiencing tremendous relief. This is a Yogic exercise, so think yourself into the position where you are actively aware of the instant relaxation it is bringing you.*

AN EXERCISE ROUTINE
FOR YOU

Raised Leg Stretch.

Torso Twist.

Leg Swing.

Waist Stretch.

Cross-over Swing.

Hip Swing One.

Scissor Stretch.

Scissor Raise.

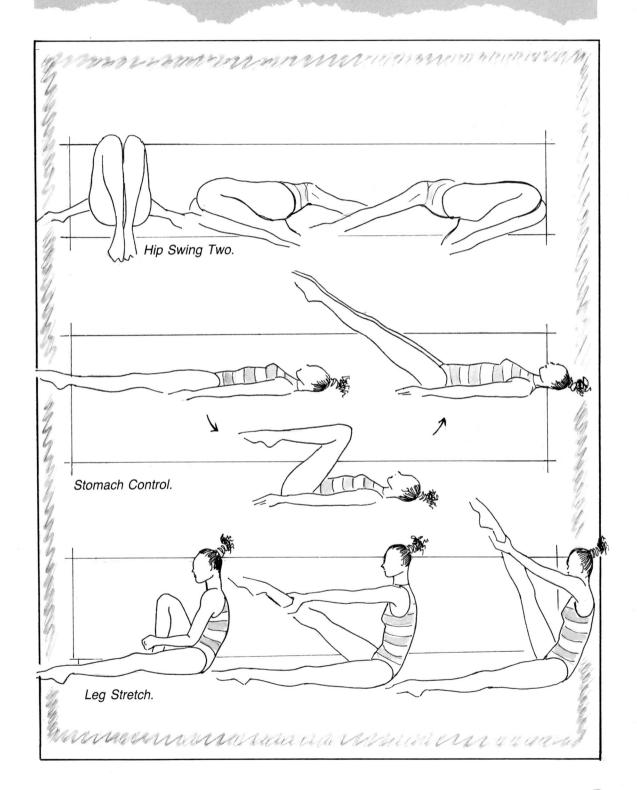

Hip Swing Two.

Stomach Control.

Leg Stretch.

CHAPTER 5

SKIN DEEP

The mystique of our beautiful skin, shining, black, supple and velvety to the touch, conveys an air of sensuality. My sister, dark skin is truly beautiful skin and its beauty goes beyond the bounds of Africa. Light-skinned sun lovers consider a tan a sign of health and beauty. It is our heritage. Caring for your skin now is an investment for the future, for it is the first line of defence against pollution and weather. The condition of your skin depends on your lifestyle and although one rarely sees a woman in rural Africa with a bad complexion, remove her to an industrialised setting, and skin problems can result. A diet high in animal fat or full of chemicals and preservatives, a body sustained by rushed meals of junk food, a lack of exercise, central heating, air conditioning and pollution – all these factors add up to the challenges of modern skin care.

Your skin reveals all your habits, whether you suffer from stress, smoke, drink alchohol, take birth control pills or eat greasy food. But don't be alarmed, although the skin is a complex structure, and there seem to be so many different products to apply to it, by determining what kind of skin you have, you can learn how best to care for it.

In it's very complexity, the skin is a fascinating protective organ for your body. Let's try to understand a little about its structure and how it functions, so that we can select those skin care products that will enhance its natural beauty.

In good condition, the skin is a glowing, supple, elastic and waterproof covering, sensitive to the touch of the lover – or – harsh chemicals. It is made up of two layers, the epidermis and the dermis. The epidermis, or outer layer, consists of dead cells which are being constantly shed, to be replaced immediately from underneath by new cells from the dermis.

On black skins the discarded outer cells of the epidermis can have that ashy appearance or a radiant bloom. Each cell has a thick fatty wall, which attracts and holds water. The amount of water the dead cells can retain determines to a large extent your skin texture, its smoothness and softness. Often this is not enough for the preservation of the flexibility of the skin.

Therefore even if we think we have an oily skin, we still need additional moisture with skin creams and lotions to help plump out the layer of dead cells, and protect the skin from the many external dangers to which it is constantly exposed.

Fortunately for us, the epidermis of black skin is tougher than that of white, containing the melanin which determines the fantastic variety of black skin colour. It also protects our skin from many diseases, (such as skin cancer and psoriasis) and gives some protection against the sun's harmful ultra-violet rays. It has a much more generous supply of sweat and oil glands, emitting their secretions on the outer surface, through tiny openings called pores. Not only are these pores larger, but the sweat they exude gives our skin that wonderful healthy sheen, which should never be treated as oiliness. It is 'The red-gold reflections on our shimmering skin,' as the great Senegalese poet, Léopold Senghor put it.

The dermis below contains a special type of protein known as collagen, together with elastic fibres. Both give the skin its suppleness and strength. In fact most Black women, unless they have had a life of unremitting suffering or starvation, are still gorgeous at 50. Under the dermis is a layer of fat, which separates the skin from the muscles, and is responsible for the curves for which we are so appreciated.

As long as the network of collagen and elastic fibres remain smooth and properly arranged, your skin will be youthful and firm; but it will start to line and sag when the fibres begin to harden, bunch up and become disorganised. Rapidly accelerated ageing could be as much a result of illness, bad diet and pollution, as the onset of middle age.

Much of the beauty and health of your skin depends on the dermis, that deeper layer which contains our blood vessels, nerves, oil and sweat glands, elastic tissues, hair follicles and tiny muscles. Problem-prevention is the wisest course, because superficial treatment is impossible. No skin care products can penetrate the waterproof epidermis to work wonders in the dermis, and if they did, they would be dangerous, as damaging this layer can cause permanent scar tissue. So don't waste your money on expensive products which make extravagant claims. Real moisture and nutrients are supplied to the dermis through your blood.

As a sense organ, the skin responds immediately to cold, heat, pain, pressure and of course to sensual stimulation. It is immediately affected by illness, black skin taking on a greyish appearance. Your skin is truly a mirror of your health and well-being, so treat it as your best friend, and take good care of it. Skin care products alone can not make you feel 'at ease' in your skin. A disciplined routine of careful facial and body skin care, combined with a balanced, nutritious diet of whole grains and fresh vegetables and fruit, together with plenty of water, fresh air, exercise, freedom from stress and protection against the environment – these are the ingredients of superb black skin. Remember too that your body needs about 8 hours sleep a night – and what will broadcast the news first about those endless late nights? Your skin!

ENEMIES OF THE SKIN

INTERNAL FOES

As we have discussed, you are what you eat and you can be your own worst enemy. I don't believe that there is any traditional, magic or modern beauty food that can give you magnificent baby skin or a rejuvenated appearance. Isabel of Bavaria, Queen of France at the end of the 14th century, was said to have enriched her complexion with a lotion of boar's brains, wolf's blood and crocodile glands! Our traditional herbalists too have some interesting preparations, which are worth investigating. But right here and now, we know that certain foods have adverse effects, while others help to improve the skin. If you have a tendency to sensitive skin, or suffer from skin allergies, you should avoid stimulants and peppery foods. These include hot peppers, spices (especially ginger), alchohol, 'ordinary' as opposed to herbal tea and coffee.

If you suffer from Acne, avoid fried, peppery, rich foods and chocolate. Food that is known to have a directly beneficial effect on the health, and therefore on the skin, includes honey, cider vinegar, fresh fruit, vegetables, cod liver oil, Vitamin E – and if you can obtain them, – the herbs, comfrey, calendula (from marigolds) and nettles.

The skin is not only a mirror of your health, but also of your emotions. Unfortunately many of us are either unaware of or do not appreciate the relationship between stress and the skin. As you know, our black skin is richer in oil glands and constant worrying can increase hormone production that overstimulates the oil glands, clogging the pores and causing pimples. Acne may worsen on the approach of an important occasion, and horror upon horror – cold sores may appear suddenly on the lips,

on the eve of marriage! Make friends with stress, practise conscious relaxation and learn to meditate, or it can destroy your skin, good looks, vitality and health.

EXTERNAL ASSAILANTS

The high melanin content in your skin won't give you full protection from the harmful rays of the sun, especially if you are light-skinned, and sunbathe without the necessary precautions. Long exposure to the sun's rays can also cause premature ageing and skin cancer. No matter how black your skin is, you should protect it when the sun is fierce, and always try to stay in the shade.

Modern central heating and air conditioning systems take away precious water from the skin, as do our desert conditions and the West African Harmattan wind, blowing off the Sahara. Have you noticed how the Harmattan can dry up wood, twisting it and bending it, so that cupboard doors no longer shut properly? This is because the moisture has gone. You need to moisturise your skin more in these conditions, even if you have an oily skin.

Air pollution is a silent enemy which makes the skin age rapidly. Most pollution is an environmental problem which can only be tackled by communal or government action – to limit the exhaust from vehicles, smoke from industry and so on. However, cigarette smoke is something we can act on, by not smoking ourselves and telling others who want to smoke in our presence that it is O.K. as long as they don't exhale! For not only is cigarette smoke linked with lung cancer and heart disease, it also makes the skin age rapidly, due to a substance found in cigarette smoke called Benzopyrene. This uses up the body's supply of Vitamin C rapidly, depriving the body's collagen of it, with the resultant wrinkling of the skin.

Excessively hot or cold water also dries the skin. Use lukewarm water when bathing.

horny layer

hair   sweat pore from sweat gland

blood vessel

living layer

epidermis

nerve endings,

dermis

muscle   hair follicle

oil gland

BLACK IS BEAUTIFUL

The basic properties of skin are the same the world over, and skin colour is genetically determined, although other factors affect the ultimate tone. Colour is determined by these main factors:-

- *Haemoglobin in the blood: an iron compound which when carrying oxygen round the body is red. It becomes blue when carrying carbon dioxide. The effect of haemoglobin is more obvious in white than in black skin, which turns red in 'blushing', when its owner is embarassed.*
- *Carotene: a yellow pigment in the fatty cells of the epidermis. It is the same pigment that is present in plants rich in Vitamin A, such as carrots.*
- *Melanin: a brownish-black pigment manufactured and distributed by special cells of the basement layer of the epidermis, called melanocytes. They originally develop from brain cells and make a long journey to your skin to give up their colour to other surrounding cells in the upper layer of the skin, to make it black and beautiful, and to protect it against the sun's damaging rays. Melanin is also present in the choroid of the eye, giving you those beautiful brown eyes.*

The factor determining whether you are white, brown, black or yellow is the activity of the melanocytes and the amount and distribution of their pigment to the other skin cells around them, which are merely carriers of the melanin. In black skin the melanocytes are more active than in white skin, and the pigment granules are larger and more evenly distributed throughout the cell, forming a strong barrier against the ultra-violet rays of the sun. But in white skin the pigments are smaller and tend to be clumped together here and there, allowing the sun's rays to penetrate deep into the skin and damage it. This is one of the reasons why white skin ages faster than black, especially if it's owner has done a lot of sun-tanning.

The way in which light is reflected or absorbed on the skin's surface depends on the amount of melanin in your skin. The lighter your skin, the more it reflects light, while the darker your colour, the more light is being absorbed into it. Adaptation of skin pigmentation is believed to be directly linked to the strength of the sun, producing (along with genetic inheritance) the infinite variety of skin colour across Africa, from the pale North Africans to the blue-blacks of Sudan and Ethiopia.

THE SHADES OF BLACK

Your skin is part of a fabulous kaleidoscope of Black skin colours.

If you look closely at your skin, you will notice a rather quieter colour or 'undertone' in addition to your main skin colour. We also have a large variety of these undertones – blue, yellow, red, orange and purple. Your skin colour may therefore be:-

- *jet black*
- *blue/black*
- *purple/black*
- *brown/red*
- *bronze*
- *honey*

and so on. Such a fantastic spectrum gives us endless scope for colour creativity in selecting our clothes, accessories and cosmetics.

SKIN TYPES

You inherit the type of skin you have for better or for worse. But there are products to enhance your good qualities and remedies for problems. However, it takes a little know-how and a regular routine to achieve the desired results. We shall group our skin types into five, but please note that skin may change from one type to the other over the years. Skin also changes when you move from one climate to another and your skin oil flows more freely in the hot sun, so don't mistake this for oily skin.

First determine your skin type and then apply the appropriate skin care. Many beauty

The blue-black tone of a Kenyan woman.

The brown-red tone of a Ghanaian woman.

The bronze tone of a Sierra Leonean woman.

The honey tone of an Eastern Nigerian woman.

The ivory tone of a Black British woman.

The yellow-brown tone of an Azanian woman.

books talk about a tissue test to determine skin type, but don't bother with this; it was developed with white skin in mind. If your skin is dry or oily, you will know, because you will feel it and see it, your facial skin being the best indicator of skin type. Though skin types may differ, every face needs cleansing, toning and moisturising in appropriate ways. Skin types range from:-

- *Normal-to-dry skin.*
- *Sensitive skin.*
- *Normal-to-oily skin.*
- *Combination skin.*
- *Normal skin.*

NORMAL-TO-DRY SKIN

'Ashiness' or whitish dry areas of our bodies, especially over the arms and legs, can result from the skin's rapid loss of moisture, caused by changes in temperature and humidity. It is quite common especially in cold climates (due to over-effective central heating) and in West Africa (during the Harmattan season) when the skin is abnormally exposed to drying conditions. It should not be mistaken for dry skin. Try to protect yourself under these conditions by using an effective moisturiser and a humidifier in your house and office.

If your facial skin is dry, while the rest of your body is normal, there may be something medically wrong, so consult your doctor or a skin specialist. Other drying elements are over-harsh soap and skin lighteners. In true normal-to-dry skin, your skin is not sufficiently lubricated, because it is not holding enough water in the surface cell layers. The upper outer arms and outer thighs may feel dry and rough to the touch, while your skin feels tight after washing, and may be flaky, with criss-cross lines all over it. If your face dries and chaps easily at the onset of cold weather in your country or the Harmattan, then you have normal-to-dry skin.

To care for dry skin, use hypo-allergenic, non-perfumed products, and above all, never use soap on your face. Soap is for floors and walls, not delicate dry skins. Cleanse with a rich cream or lotion, removing gently and thoroughly. Use an alchohol-free toner or cold water to remove all traces of cleanser. Obviously moisturising is more important for this skin type than any other, so in the daytime, use a liquid oil-based moisturiser, and at night a rich cream one, aiming for the type that is absorbed into the skin, if you don't want to put off your partner!

▶ SENSITIVE SKIN ◀

This type of skin is usually normal-to-dry, but can sometimes be excessively oily. It develops allergies to food and cosmetics and is prone to itchiness and spots. Such skin suffers more when subjected to external and internal sources of damage than any other. Even using someone else's soap or powder puff can bring the skin out in a rash.

Be on your guard against any kind of skin care or cosmetic preparation containing perfume or additives, so read labels carefully and go for hypo-allergenic products. Try using baby lotions and soaps for the body, baby oil for cleansing the face, and witch-hazel for toning.

NORMAL-TO-OILY SKIN

When white skin is oily, it shines; when black skin shines, it looks great. It is only when the sheer bulk of highly packed oil glands give black skin a thickened and coarse appearance, with large easily visible pores, that oily skin becomes greasy skin. When it's greasy, the shine is over-evident, and this type of skin is the one prone to acne, spots, blackheads and whiteheads.

So be sure that your naturally glowing 'shining' skin is not dried out by being treated as if it were over oily, especially if the cleansers and toners contain acetone, developed for white skins.

Naturally oily skin ages well, but meanwhile, before extreme old age, cleansing and yet more cleansing is the answer for you! Wash your face frequently with a mild soap or cleansing bar, but never with the perfumed or medicated soap you use on your body. Occasionally try an anti-bacterial soap, more frequently if you have Acne. Always use a clean face cloth, complexion brush or natural sponge. Otherwise, use a cleansing lotion specially formulated for black skins, of the non-greasy milk variety. Baby oil is also effective in removing make-up. To avoid blackheads, try using cleansing grains or a 'facial sponge' once a week.

Tone with an astringent formulated for 'normal' white skins, or a special one for Acne. Often strong toners are recommended for people with oily skins, but be careful. Remember that oil-removing procedures used repeatedly can so easily upset the moisture balance of your skin. Oil is one thing, moisture quite another. Again, black skins are believed to suffer less from allergies, due to their extra melanin content, but it is so easy to set up an allergy or severe irritation by scrubbing away with abrasive lotions.

You too need to moisturise your skin, though not with creams containing high amounts of glycerine or mineral oil. Try to obtain products containing vegetable fats, like groundnut or coconut. Choose a light non-greasy, water-based moisturiser, using it night and morning. Before putting on make-up, allow the moisturiser to dry for ten minutes, blotting off any excess with a tissue. There are special moisturisers for Acne-sufferers.

COMBINATION SKIN

This is our most common skin type, which I was tempted to classify under 'Normal'. It is usually normal-to-oily in the T-zone area of the face (forehead, nose and chin) and a little drier on the cheeks, around the eyes and throat. Some people have a combination of oily and more oily. In this case, use an astringent to control the shine, and avoid heavy make-up, which can clog the pores.

Cleanse with a mild complexion soap, using a facial sponge, or a mild liquid cleanser or water-soluble cream. Tone the oilier T-zone with an astringent or witch-hazel, and for your cheeks and throat, try one of the flower-water toners, such as rose-water or orange-flower-water, or use cold water.

Again, if you can obtain them, moisturise with light cream preparations containing yarrow and comfrey, the latter a plant which has been used since the 12th century for its natural healing properties. Apply less moisturiser to the T-zone area.

NORMAL SKIN

The envy of us all. Your skin is perfectly balanced, looks healthy and smooth, not too oily nor too dry, with no enlarged pores, and not a spot in sight. Cleanse, tone and moisturise your skin as for a combination type, but stay away from heavy make-up. A velvet complexion like yours needs no covering up, and it is all too easy to take a skin that causes no problems for granted. Conditions such as pregnancy or stress can upset normal skin-balance, so take especially good care of your precious asset.

New ranges of products come on the international market now and again all claiming to do wonderful things for your skin. Note that most of them are formulated with white skin in mind, and grouping of skin types being not quite the same, you may be cleansing your skin too harshly, using the wrong products.

● FACIAL SKIN CARE

As we have seen, the effective approach to facial skin care is a regular beauty plan of:-

- *cleansing*
- *toning*
- *moisturising*
- *make-up.*

Remember these general guidelines for facial skin care:-

- *Find the type of soap or cleanser that suits you and stick to it, especially if you have a sensitive skin.*
- *To reduce the risk of spots or infection, keep your hands off your face as much as possible, and always wash your hands before caring for your face. Keep all soaps and towels used for your face separate from the ones you use for your body, and wash the towels and washcloths frequently and seperately from ordinary laundry.*
- *Apply all lotions and creams to your face with clean fingers, clean cotton wool swabs, or tissues.*

- *Establish a regular routine of skin care, morning and night, and stick to it, no matter how tired or busy you may be. Spasmodic skin care is a waste of time, and produces no results.*
- *Never use hot water on your face.*
- *Make sure your wash basin is cleaned frequently and rinsed well with a mild disinfectant. Alternatively, have a separate face wash bowl for your use alone, though of course it must be kept equally clean.*
- *Don't leave your make-up on for more than eight hours. Remove it completely and re-apply if you need to. If you are going to be at home in the evening, or not going out during the day, give your skin a holiday by wearing moisturiser alone.*
- *Those of us who live in tropical climates should remember that cosmetics and skin care products deteriorate very fast in the heat, especially when packaged in plastic (as opposed to jars.) Keep them in the fridge, and ensure that all lids are tightly closed.*

CLEANSING

We cleanse to get rid of the film of grease, dead skin cells, dried sweat residue, accumulated dirt, a few germs and of course, make-up, if you wear it. It is not only water that rids the face of these things; in fact too much soap and water can be dangerous, as it dissolves away the protective fatty walls of the skin cells, leaving your poor skin dry, flaky and sore.

Grease can be dissolved in grease, which is why there are cleansing agents in the form of creams, lotions and bars. These contain mineral oils and ingredients that break up and remove dirt and make-up from the orifices of the sebacous glands. They are available according to skin type. Cleansers low in oils (suitable for oily skin) are called 'milks.' Those high in oil content are called 'creams.' An 'emulsion' comes between the two, for normal skins.

TONING

After cleansing your face, it is very refreshing to use products known as 'toners', 'fresheners' or 'astringents.' Some of these contain alchohol or similar substances, together with water and glycerine. They evaporate very quickly and the sensation produced is one of coolness and slight tingling, that give a feeling of freshness and cleanliness; hence their appeal. Their main function, however, is to act as a mild antiseptic, dissolving away any residual traces of grease, dirt, or the remains of your cleansing agent. They help to seal the pores, especially if you have a greasy skin. In this case, buy one with a higher alchohol content, usually called an astringent.

Choose the toning lotion according to your skin type, avoiding any that contain over 20% of alchohol, since even if you consider yours to be an oily skin, an excess of alchohol deprives it of moisture, especially in the delicate age-revealing areas around the eyes. Simply splashing your face with cold water after cleansing also has a toning effect.

MOISTURISING AND CONDITIONING CREAMS/LOTIONS

This is the final stage in the skin care process, designed to preserve the skin against ageing and the environment, and to prepare it for the glamourising process of make-up. Some moisturisers are emulsions of 'water-in-oil', as rich creams for night use, or in a lighter version for the day, for dry skins. They protect against excessive water loss into the atmosphere by trapping the water in the outer layer of the skin. The other types are the 'oil-in-water' varieties, which are less greasy, suitable for day or night use for most skin types.

All types of skin need moisturisers, but at best they are only fighting a delaying action in the ageing process. The value of good moisturisers is to help maintain the water balance of the skin; help protect it against pollution; and help make the skin's texture feel softer.

Tinted moisturisers are best applied *over* your basic one, as they contain chemicals used in the colouring, which are harmful in direct contact with the skin.

● DAILY BEAUTY ROUTINE

REQUIREMENTS

Cleansing agent, toner, moisturiser, night cream, face flannel, cotton wool, tissues or nappy liners, facial sponge or baby sponge, face towel and water.

METHOD

- *Tie your hair back with a scarf.*
- *Wet the face with luke-warm water, if using soap or cleansing bar.*
- *Work the cleanser (cream, liquid or soap) gently into the skin in an upward circular motion, using both hands (the tendency is to use only your right hand.) In this way you are giving your face a massage at the same time.*
- *If using cream or lotion, clean off the cleansing agent with a tissue, massaging the face gently with the same movements.*
- *If using soap, massage the lather into*

your face or use a complexion brush. Then rinse off with plenty of lukewarm water, and pat dry with a clean face towel.

- *Apply the toner, using cotton wool swabs, paying attention to the more oily areas and using less on the drier parts e.g. under and around the eyes. Make sure that you remove all traces of the cleanser, or your skin will become irritated or dry.*
- *In the morning, feed your skin with moisturiser, while it is still slightly damp. Pour a little onto your hand and dot the moisturiser all over your face and neck. With your fingers, lightly rub it into your face with the usual movements, letting your skin absorb it by itself, rather than rubbing too much.*
- *If your skin is dry or ageing, use a night cream in the same way. Many older women like to use an eye cream, an effective concentration of active ingredients, providing intensive care for that fragile area around the eyes. Choose one that is easily absorbed, and does not leave any oily residue.*

FACIAL MASSAGE

This does wonders for facial skin if performed properly and regularly. It soothes the facial nerve supply, which promotes the elimination of waste products and absorption of nutrients and the active ingredients of the oils and creams by the skin cells. This makes your skin more elastic and young-looking.

METHOD

Most movements are repeated five times on a face and neck smothered with cream or oil. Any pure vegetable oil will do, such as olive oil, corn oil or sunflower oil. Use gentle flowing upward movements to counteract the natural tendency of the facial skin and muscles to droop.

Neck and chin

Begin massaging from the neck to stimulate the

blood supply to the face. Place your left hand on your right collar bone, sweep your hand upwards across the neck, up the side of the face to the right ear. Do the same for the other side, using your right hand.

Massage the back of your neck upwards to the hair line. Bring one hand and then the other round the neck from the back across the front to massage the neck.

Jaws

To release tension around the jaws, which can soon pull down the corners of the mouth. One at a time, bring each hand upwards from the sides of the neck, over the front, under the chin and outward over the jawbone to the ears. Then stroke upwards from the corners of the mouth to the temples.

With the first two fingers of each hand, simultaneously work upwards on the jaw bone from the chin to the ears, using gentle spiralling movements.

Upper cheeks

With soft stroking movements, using the finger tips of three fingers resting on the nose, sweep both hands across the cheek bone to the ears. This is very good for your cheek bones, releasing tension from your face.

Lower cheeks

Using the first two fingers of each hand, work upwards in the same spiralling motion from the sides of your nose to the upper corner of your cheek bone. This helps delay the drooping of the lower cheek area.

Mouth

Using the forefinger of one hand, go round and round the mouth, first in one direction, then the other. This helps to prevent laugh lines.

Eyes

The skin around the eyes is thin and delicate, so use very gentle movements. Apply a little more oil or cream and with your third finger (for less pressure) stroke around both eyes

simultaneously, circling around the eyes gently, beginning from the inner corners. Finish with tiny circles towards the ears in the areas between the outer corners of the eyes to the hair line.

Forehead

Using the flat part of three fingers of both hands, massage upwards from the bridge of the nose in curving lines away from the centre of the forehead towards the hair line. This helps to iron out those frown lines. But then you could stop frowning!

Finally, with the tips of the fingers, tap lightly several times all over the chin, jaws, over the upper and lower cheeks in an upward and outward direction and also across the forehead. You should feel a warm tingling sensation, as the blood flow is stimulated.

Remove the excess oil with a tissue with upward movements, never downwards, and splash your face several times with cold water, patting your face dry with a towel. In hot climates, you can add ice cubes to the tap water. Now take a look at your face in the mirror. You should be pleased with its tone and freshness.

Use the massage movements as you cleanse your face, and give yourself a thorough massage two or three times a week, preferably at night.

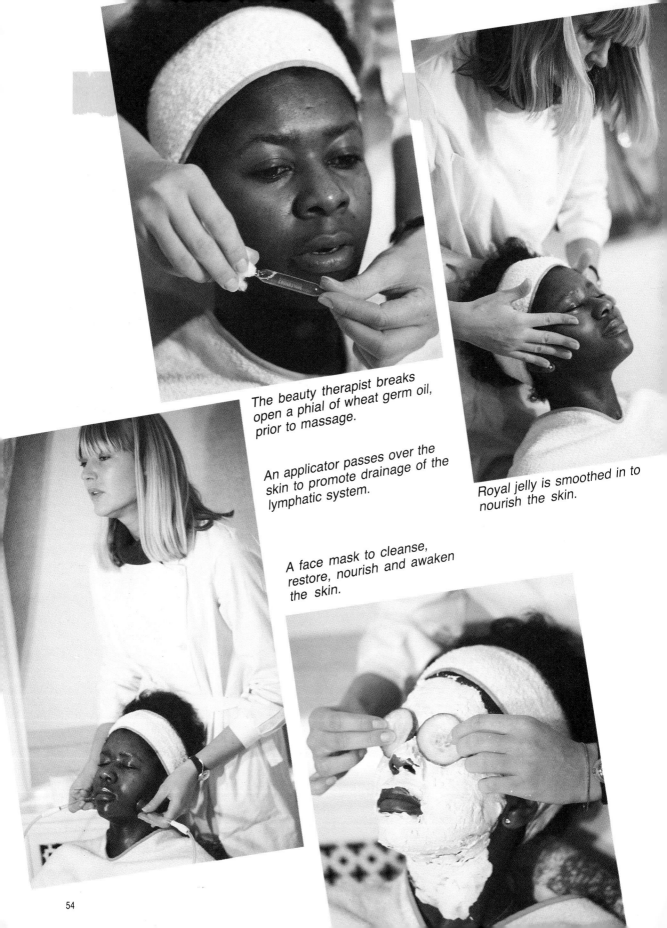

The beauty therapist breaks open a phial of wheat germ oil, prior to massage.

An applicator passes over the skin to promote drainage of the lymphatic system.

Royal jelly is smoothed in to nourish the skin.

A face mask to cleanse, restore, nourish and awaken the skin.

FACIAL MASKS

Masks have been used by women for thousands of years; Egyptian women at the time of the Pharoes applied clay to rejuvenate their skin. To this day, a trip to a health spa or beauty salon can be an eye-opener, women covered from head to toe in restorative green mud!

Although skin-care masks will not work instant miracles on skin which is really out of condition – this requires habitual, patient treatment – masks certainly have a beneficial effect. They can also give you a tremendous, pampered feeling, a temporary lift for a special occasion.

When used regularly, facial masks have a definite therapeutic effect, working in various ways, according to your skin type:-

- *Peel-off, medicated masks remove surface dead cells, unclog pores and carry away accumulated impurities, excellent for lifeless or oily skin.*
- *Moisturising creams and gels, soothing and enriching dry and ageing skin.*
- *Stimulating masks, some soothing, others mentholated. Choose the right sort for your skin, and you will experience an essentially temporary lift of a sparkling youthful skin, with tightened pores and firmed-up contours. Great before a party.*

  Obviously it is essential to choose the correct mask for your skin-type, applying it every ten days or so, if yours is a dry skin, more frequently if oily. The same method of application applies to everyone:-
- *Stroke on some moisturiser.*
- *Open the skin pores by bending over a steaming bowl of boiling water for about seven minutes, with a towel draped over your head, to maximise the effect. You can enhance the process by putting healing herbs into the water, traditionally-used ones in Africa or the West Indies, or comfrey, calendula or elderflower if you live in temperate climates.*
- *If you are using a commercial preparation, follow the manufacturer's instructions. But if you are making your own mask, don't place it around your eyes. This delicate area should be covered with some moisturiser or a couple of slices of cucumber.*
- *After application, use the time it takes for the mask to work as a positive relaxation time. Lie flat on your back, and retreat into your inner space, contemplating if you like, the beautiful things you are doing for your beautiful self.*

HOME-MADE MASKS

Some of the most effective masks are prepared with natural, easily obtainable ingredients; so don't despair if you can't get hold of expensive commercially produced ones. Here are some that African women have been using for centuries:-

Avocado mask

The Avocado is one of the most nutritious vegetables for the care of your body, both internally and externally, and grows in many parts of the Tropics. It contains several vitamins, minerals and natural oils and is good for all types of skin, most particularly for dry skin. Eat it regularly and don't throw away the skin. Most of the vegetable's nutritional value lies in that dark green layer just beneath the skin.

    2 tablespoons ripe avocado pear (including the greenest part under the skin.)
    1 teaspoon liquid honey.
    2 drops of lemon juice.

Mash the avocado pear into a smooth paste with the lemon juice, to prevent it going black. Add the honey and mix thoroughly. Apply evenly to your face and around your eyes. Leave for fifteen minutes, then wash off with lukewarm water. You can also spread the paste all over your body, to moisturise and nourish the skin.

Egg yolk mask

The protein and lecithin in the yolk is also very nourishing for the skin.

    1 egg yolk. (Choose a large fresh egg.)
    1 teaspoon vegetable oil (olive or almond.)
    Just mix together and apply to the face.
Leave for twenty minutes, then rinse off.

Egg and lemon mask

This mask is for greasy or normal-to-oily skin.

    1 Fresh egg yolk.
    1 teaspoon of honey.
    1 teaspoon of pure olive oil.
    juice of ½ a lemon.
    Drop the egg yolk into the squeezed lemon juice and leave for twenty minutes to allow time for the lemon oils to be absorbed by the egg. Mix in the honey and oil and apply to the face.

SKIN PROBLEMS

PIGMENT LOSS OR LIGHT PATCHES

This is common throughout the world, but in our case, is more evident, and unhappily, the cause is unknown. Light patches are sometimes caused by mild fungus infections of the skin, common in warm, humid climates. So consult your doctor. Loss of colour or Vitiligo may first be noticed on the back of the hands or the face. Apart from eating more liver or the supplement Paba, the only solution is camouflage, by blending in carefully selected make-up. Avoid tanning, because the lighter patches will be more obvious.

DARK PATCHES, INCREASED PIGMENT

During pregnancy or while taking birth control pills, black women often develop darker pigmentation along the centre of the face, which can be quite disturbing, as it sometimes takes a long time to fade, or may not fade completely. You should consult your doctor immediately. If your skin does not return to normal, I'm afraid you too will have to resort to clever use of make-up.

SKIN BLEACHING

Now this is a self-inflicted problem. Why bleach? Today, 'Black is beautiful', and yet some of us still bleach. The active ingredient in the bleaching cream is very harmful to the body, interfering with its normal healing properties. It also destroys the melanocytes and their pigment melanin, resulting in a loss of protection against the sun. Those of you who still bleach today should realise that you are seriously endangering your health.

    Fade creams also inhibit the production of melanin, thus rendering you liable to serious sunburn.

KELOIDS

Black skin is over-enthusiastic in healing, and when our skin is damaged or broken, a thickened dark growth of fibrous tissue, usually larger than the original wound develops. A keloid can sometimes be ugly, and it can form where there has been no external skin damage, for example on the chest, where heavy, unsupported breasts pull on the skin over the chest-bone. If you are considering cosmetic surgery on your face or want to have your ears pierced, remember that there is always the risk of keloid formation.

Treatment includes X-rays, steroid injections or surgery, all of which are potentially dangerous.

ACNE

A painful skin disorder, associated with very oily skin, but not limited to young people, nor of course, to blacks. But because black skin is more prone to scarring and acne is so common, it is discussed in this book, whereas rarer skin problems are more the province of the medical profession.

Acne is an infection of the sebaceous (oil) glands, most common among teenagers, due to the hormonal changes associated with adolescence. It usually appears at around twelve to thirteen years and reaches its peak by seventeen to eighteen years, after which it should slowly settle down and disappear. But sometimes it continues into the thirties, and these teenage spots can be very embarassing! Hormonal changes in pregnancy or while taking oral contraceptives can also bring on the condition in an adult.

Acne is caused by the over-production of sebum (oil), and usually when levels of two growth hormones, Progesterone and Testosterone are high. The Testosterone is a male hormone also present in women, though in smaller quantities. This hormone stimulates the sebaceous glands to increase their sebum production and a thick plug of grease and dirt fills the duct, the familiar 'whitehead.' It turns dark when it meets the air, as it contains the tanning pigment melanin. A blackhead is born!

When these become infected, the surrounding areas are inflamed and angry-looking. Hence the pimple or spot. If promptly and effectively treated at this stage, there should be no scarring. In some severe cases, the walls of the infected duct burst and infection deep down in the skin occurs, causing cystic lesions, which leave permanent scars after the infection has healed.

Prevention is better than cure

Although it is difficult to actually control the production of excessive sebum, you can help yourself by reducing the amount of rich, fatty, peppery foods you eat, and by eating more foods high in Vitamins A and C. But you must keep the skin clean, removing dirt and grease regularly and learning to live with stress, which can cause a flare-up. And remember that regular exercise does help to cleanse the skin of waste products.

Treatment of acne

Good news! The high humidity and heat in the coastal areas of the Tropics, with the increased resultant activity of our sweat glands, keep our pores open, and help keep acne at bay. But if acne does strike, it soon deteriorates dramatically due to these conditions. Although it is unsightly, acne is more a medical than a cosmetic problem. But it is painful and should not be treated harshly.

For mild acne

Try self-help first. There are many anti-bacterial soaps, cleansing grains and medicated lotions for acne. If they are available where you live, try them, but avoid the harsh ones that strip your skin. After cleansing, to remove more dirt, grease and dead surface cells, you can also give your face a gentle scrub with sea-salt. Sprinkle a little on a clean wet face-cloth, and apply for two minutes using delicate circular and upward motions as for cleansing. Rinse and moisturise. Avoid greasy moisturisers or foundation creams. Use the facial scrub twice a week and with the right preventive regime, your acne should improve. Please don't use heavy make-up to conceal acne, as this only further clogs up the pores, and never leave make-up on at night. In severe cases, consult your doctor who may prescribe antibiotics, hormone treatment or hopefully homeopathic or herbal treatments, as you can't be pushing antibiotics and hormones into your system on a long-term basis – the symptoms will not be cured, only suppressed.

BODY SKIN CARE

'The way to health is to have an aromatic bath and a scented massage every day' wrote Hippocrates.

Those precious few moments of daily body care are often the only time which some really busy women devote completely to their own well-being. Don't spend all your time and money on your face, and then neglect your body. That precious body shows age and responds to regular care, just as your face does. Body care is based on the same simple regular routine of gentle cleansing, thorough rinsing, drying and moisturising.

SHOWERS

Many beauty books speak of a relaxing soak in the bath, but this may not always be possible. In some parts and some seasons in Africa, water is scarce, so be thoughtful in your use of this precious commodity. Showers are also a quick and effective way to get your whole body clean, without wallowing in the dirt that comes off it! Another advantage of a shower is the stimulating effect of the water pressure, making the skin tingle and glow, and improving your circulation. You can wash your hair at the same time, thereby saving that precious water.

Your bath or shower water should not be too hot nor too cold, to avoid skin damage. A good body scrub stimulates the skin, cleans out the dirt and helps to remove the dead surface skin cells. Use an African vegetable sponge (coils of fibre produced by beating certain creepers, but take care as they may block your drains), a natural sponge or a loofah. A wash cloth can never do the job as well. Go over the horny parts – elbows, feet and knees – with a brush.

Avoid over-harsh soap, especially if your skin is sensitive. Baby and non-perfumed soaps are good for all skin types.

Relaxing in a scented, moisturising bath.

BATHS

If you prefer the relaxing qualities of a bath, don't sit too long in it, as your skin can become water-logged (it will look crinkly at the toes and fingers.) Soaking in a bath full of soapy, alkaline water is not beneficial to your skin, so soap and rinse at the end of your bath, having luxuriated in some wonderful scented bath oil. Other therapeutic bath additives include bicarbonate of soda for an irritated skin; Epsom salts or oatmeal to soften the water; sea-salt or household starch to soothe tired muscles; and relaxing herbs such as camomile or your local equivalent.

Make sure you rinse off all the soap because any residue can cause dryness or ashiness. If you can bear it, a splash of cold water will close the pores as well as any skin tonic. Then dry your body properly, paying attention to the folds of the skin, and moisturise quickly, while the skin is still a little damp.

For the true hedonist, you don't really need to emulate Cleopatra, with her bath of asses' milk. The key is your soothing bath oil, with nourishing moisturising lotion, a puff of talcum powder and a spray of cologne. Caress your whole body with tender, loving care! Finally, before stepping out for a big night out, apply some perfume, (though not on your evening dress.)

A spray of perfume matching your bath oil and talc puts you in a mood to celebrate.

CHAPTER 6

THE ART OF MAKE-UP

You are the artist; your face is the canvas. There is no such thing as the archetypal Black Beauty, so the preparations you put on your face, their contouring and colours will be as individual as the unique beauty you are.

While facial features differ according to racial characteristics, what you do with your life reveals itself in your face in much the same way all over the world. When we are young and problem free, there is hardly any story for our faces to tell. But as time goes by, the experiences of life, whether fulfilling or frustrating, all leave their mark. Wherever you live and whatever your age – but particularly as the years roll by – certain characteristics are manifestly evident in your face. These are good humour, serenity, kindness and purity of thought and action.

It goes without saying that the canvas on which you, the artist, will set to work, reflects your health, diet and the skin care you have been applying, according to its type. The facial bones you inherited give your face its unique shape and structure. But your facial muscles and skin texture are constantly changing, for better or worse, and these you can do something about. Before taking up your palette, remember that the bones of the face are covered by a network of very intricate muscles, which gradually register the amount of frowning, smiling or tensing up that we subject them to.

FACIAL TYPES

The traditional African sculpture that nowadays fetches such high prices at international art auctions reveals various classical face shapes, which change according to the area of the continent. Now that Blacks have dispersed all over the world, intermarrying with the local people, other facial shapes and characteristics have been added. These types include:-

- *The round face celebrated by Yoruba sculpture.*
- *The long face of Dogon (Mali) carving.*
- *The heart-shaped face so many Ghanaian women possess.*
- *The oval face considered to be the contemporary ideal of beauty.*
- *The square face.*

A round face.

A long face.

A heart-shaped face.

An oval face.

A square face.

In facial characteristics, no cliché is as well-founded as: 'Beauty is in the eye of the beholder.' The Australian Aborigines for instance, forcibly flatten the noses of their babies, either by lying the baby face down on a hard surface, or by direct pressure with the palm of the hand.

Since it would be a dull world if every face shape looked alike, unless you are preparing yourself for a stage appearance, to be seen at a distance and under special lighting, re-contouring your face is going to give you a very over made-up appearance. You can do a whole number of things using tones and colours to correct so-called ugly features or emphasise good ones. But why look like a painted doll? You are whom you are. Perhaps the one exception is playing up your cheekbones with blusher, no matter what your facial type. In fact, blusher is a very important cosmetic, which a Black woman can use to enhance her natural beauty.

A Western make-up base prior to African make-up.

4 or 5 different powder eye-shadows applied with the finger or pencil top.

TRADITIONAL AFRICAN MAKE-UP

Since time immemorial African women (and men) have been creatively expressing themselves in wonderful designs on their faces and bodies. These include fantasy re-contouring, which interestingly enough, usually plays up negroid features. Starting with the principles of light and dark, why don't you try a special make-up for an evening out? Whichever part of your face you want to emphasise, apply a light colour, such as to a small chin, or to the top outer corner of your eyebrows, thereby balancing up features you feel could do with some improvement. Minimise a square jaw or bulging inner corners of your eyes, with dark tones. Study the artistry of such people as the Nubians, or invent your own designs.

The ingenuity and knowledge of rural African women in the use of local plants for cosmetics, skin and hair care is impressive. Gathering herbs, seeds and bark, they produced oils, dyes, powders, stains and paints for the dual purposes of ornamentation and religion or magic. Local 'Kohl' outlined the eyes to deepen their mystery and attraction, and more practically – to ward off flies and cool the eyes. Paint was also used around the eyes to ward off evil. Some eye-liners were considered love charms, making the wearer irresistible.

Many of these products are still widely available from local market stalls. Experiment with them, testing for potential rashes, by applying first to your inner wrist. It is unlikely that you will be trying the dyes used in face and body scarification or tatoos, but who knows in which direction fashion will head? Traditionally, many African children were decorated in this way, in patterns that have spiritual and tribal significance, as well as to enhance their beauty. But unless these practises are carried out hygenically, they are naturally extremely dangerous, causing serious infections and even tetanus. You should also accept that once in place, they are impossible to remove, and any attempt to do so may result in keloids.

We have reason to be proud of and grateful for our African heritage. It was due to the marks on his father's face, that my great grand-father was able to trace his roots back from the U.S.A. to Abeokuta in Nigeria and return home.

Ibilola Hoga, a dancer from Cameroon, who used to perform with Fela Anikulapo Kuti, demonstrates how to apply African make-up. 'Most of the time, one has the designs in mind before one starts,' she said. 'It's quite personal, depending on one's mood. This design is soft, and different from one side of the face to the other.'

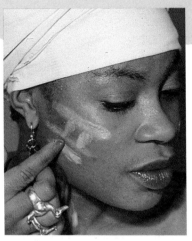

Black eyebrow pencil is used to make designs.

The design can vary from one side of the face to the other.

Applied with a matchstick, this is 'Efun' or spiritual powder, obtained from rivers, in which spirits live.

'Most of the time one has the design in mind before one starts' – Ibilola.

Spiritual powder is bought in block form from markets, then ground and mixed with water.

To finish the design, more eyebrow pencil around the mouth.

The finished effect.

BEWARE OF FAKES

Although it is informative and fun to try out traditional cosmetics from the traders' stalls, if you are buying commercial preparations, get them from a reputable chemist or department store, and even then, examine their labels very carefully. More and more fakes, especially in the foundation and hair-care product range, are appearing on the streets in Africa, and it is often difficult to detect the difference between the genuine product and its potentially harmful imitation. But copies are usually less expensive and smell cheaper too! In hot climates, check the condition of the product as well.

Test any product, whether commercial or traditional on your inner wrist for irritation. This is essential if you have a sensitive skin, but for anyone – better a rash on your arm, than on your face! You can also test for colours when selecting foundations or shadows, if the colour is the same on your face as your inner arm. The assistant at a reputable store should always be able to provide you with testers. If after a few days' use of a product, you notice any abnormality, such as a rash, irritation or swelling, stop using it immediately. Cleanse and moisturise your skin, and leave it alone, without any make-up, for a few days, to rest.

EXPERIMENTING WITH MAKE-UP

Although some young girls with perfect skin and even features look naturally beautiful without make-up, for the rest of us, the vast majority of the human species, make-up was invented to *improve* what you already have. Its psychological effect is not to be under-estimated in lifting the morale, and enhancing the user's self-esteem. But above all, make-up is fun; and it is a creative activity. Choosing the colours and tones that highlight an outfit, applying them in a masterly way, is one of the joys of being a woman.

Do you have one of those old-fashioned/idealistic partners who say that you look good 'without all that stuff on your face?' But did you notice that he almost had an accident the other day, when he saw a stunning well made-up young woman on the other side of the road? Don't think that make-up is being 'white' or 'Westernised'; you are following in the traditions of your ancestors.

Now that you have decided to take a fresh look at yourself, either by starting to wear make-up, or by changing your image, take time to examine what effect you want to achieve.

The Nigerian musician Fela Anikulapo Kuti's Queens or wives, performing in African make-up and jewellery, beaded hair and a contemporary version of the Yoruba blouse and wrapper.

Daylight make-up, soft and natural.

Artificial light make-up, dramatic with glossy eyeshadow and matching lipstick.

Before rushing out to buy a whole load of expensive products, sit down and take a look at yourself objectively in a well-lit mirror. Don't wear any make-up, so that you can observe the texture of your skin and the contours of your face, the condition of your eyes and any blemishes or lines.

While your face may not be perfect in all respects, take time to see the inherent beauty in your features, which you may never have appreciated before. Beauty magazines, friends and experts can give you advice, but you know yourself better than ever they can. Don't start experimenting with new make-up just before an evening out; first practise techniques and try out different colours of various types of make-up in the privacy of your own room, and with that vital factor – humour – you can learn to play up your best characteristics. All you can lose is some tissues and cleanser!

APPROPRIATE LIGHTING

Artificial and natural lighting have a different colour balance and intensity and therefore different effects on make-up. So always apply make-up in the same kind of light in which you

will be seen. Daytime make-up should be applied out of direct sunlight, but as near to a window as possible. Don't wear as much make-up as at night, because day-light will expose every detail, making it look very obvious and painted, if you use a thick base and over-bright tones. Daylight is blue light compared to the orange tone of electricity, so watch the changes in tone, as you move from one light source to another. Avoid making-up in fluorescent light.

Nighttime is fantasy time for make-up. You can really splurge out on wild bright colours, metallic glints, sparkling foundations and gloss.

THE ARTIST'S TOOLS

Cosmetics consist of:– foundation or base, cover stick for blemishes, blusher (or rouge), high-lighter, powder, eye-shadow, eye-liner or pencil, eyebrow pencil, mascara, lip-liner pencil, lipstick, lip gloss, nail varnish and remover.

Obviously you don't need to buy everything at once, nor do you need to invest in the following tools simultaneously. But good tools help good artists, so here goes:-

BRUSHES

The best are soft, last well and made from sable.
- *1 large powder brush with a fat rounded tip to dust off excess powder.*
- *2 smaller contour brushes, for applying blusher and highlighter.*
- *2 small brushes for eyeshadow. (Many eyeshadows and blushers come with their own little padded wands, but these don't last long, and you will notice that the professional make-up experts use brushes.)*
- *A fine lip brush. This is the most controlled way to apply lipstick, and enables you to finish off the lipstick, without wasting any.*

MORE TOOLS OF THE TRADE

- *2 lip liner pencils a shade darker than your lipstick for outlining your mouth, before filling in with lipstick. One should be on the cold blue-based side of the colour spectrum, ie a dark pink; the other on the warm brownish/red side, to match up with the warm or cold tones of your lipstick and outfit. If you have a very dark skin, you are probably better suited with a soft dark brown pencil.*
- *Eyebrow brush. These are small, flat and stiff and can also be used for separating lashes after applying mascara. They are obtainable from those old-fashioned cake mascaras.*
- *Eyebrow pencil. The professionals use two for a really soft, natural finish. Try dark brown and grey.*
- *Eyebrow tweezers.*
- *2 sponges for applying foundation, one for each tone of day and night make-up. Natural ones give a more even finish than rubber ones.*

Effective use of the tools of the trade.

- *White facial tissues or nappy liners.*
- *Absorbent cotton wool. If you are unable to obtain make-up brushes, you can improvise with cotton wool, by fixing the desired shape and size of cotton wool bud onto the end of an empty ball-point pen. This forms a working head, which is best fixed by winding round with sticky tape.*
- *A small plastic cape.*

CARE OF MAKE-UP EQUIPMENT

To avoid spots or irritation and to achieve a fresh, smooth make-up, cleanliness is the watchword. Wash your brushes, sponges and powder puffs once a fortnight, in hot soapy water to which a few drops of antiseptic have been added. Then rinse thoroughly in lukewarm water, squeeze gently and dry on a clean towel or tissue. Store them in small clean plastic bags, to protect them from dust.
Store your tweezers in a small uncovered jar with the tips standing in about an inch of equal parts of methylated spirit and water, or any mild antiseptic. Rinse off thoroughly before use.

STORING YOUR MAKE-UP

Store products that can be affected by heat, such as lipsticks and moisturisers in the fridge, in plastic bags. 'Go to town' and have a small cosmetics box made, with a lid, and compartments of different shapes for your cosmetics and brushes. Remember to hide it from your children, other members of your family and friends!

Sharpen your pencils regularly with a pencil sharpener or a one-sided blade. Never use the same blade which has been sharpening lead pencils, as the lead is poisonous. Keep the tops on the pencils, when not in use.

Clean out and disinfect your cosmetics shelf, box or drawer frequently.

COSMETICS AT WORK
CONCEALERS OR COVER-STICK

Before you begin to play with colours on your cleansed and moisturised face, first deal with any problems that you want to cover, such as an uneven skin colour, or shadows under the eyes. Concealers of the right shade and texture for your skin can help to disguise these flaws. They come in sticks, creams or cakes. The stick type is easiest to apply for small areas, but don't use it to cover raw pimples, as they may become irritated or further infected. Wait until they are healed, or at least drier.

FOUNDATION OR BASE

As the name implies, this is used to produce a smooth, flawless and even-coloured complexion. If you are very young and don't suffer from teenage blemishes, or you have really wonderful skin, you may not need foundation, though you will find that eyeshadow and blusher are blended much more effectively on a base. If you are not using foundation, the extremely light sport creams are splendid for the day-time, or indeed any time, if you don't like a made-up look. But remember to always apply a moisturiser first, whatever you do.

Foundation exists in cream, gel or liquid format, the latter being the easiest to blend in and complements the glow or natural shine of our black skin. Bear in mind that a good foundation is the basis for your make-up the whole day (or night) through, and therefore quality counts.

Cosmetic manufacturers have finally 'discovered' black skins, and are out to exploit the market. However, their gain is yours too, since you can finally take advantage of a wide variety of choice for most skin tones. Choose your base according to your skin tone and type. Oily skins need an oil-free, water-based foundation, while dry and ageing skins require a creamy type or oil-based liquid one.

Sometimes it may be difficult to get a base to match your skin exactly; its tone may fall

Apply foundation lightly and evenly with a dampened sponge.

between two foundation colours. So you may have to mix two of them. This is easily done with liquid foundation. Mix the two colours well on the back of your hand first, then apply and examine in the daylight. You may find that the foundation that looks stunning and sophisticated at night becomes an orange mask in the daytime, so your initial purchases may be several. But take heart, if you have chosen wisely, perhaps with the unbiased help of a friend, foundations last a long time.

Climatic changes

Whatever your skin type, if you are moving from a hot to a cold climate, or through the seasonal changes in Africa, you should modify your foundation type accordingly. With oily skin, use cake foundation in hot climates, but during cooler weather or winter, switch to liquid foundation to counteract the drying effect. Likewise, dry skin needs less creamy foundation when in the heat. A simple bronzing gel swept upwards over the throat, cheekbones and forehead, looks fantastic in the heat.

THE ARTIST AT WORK WITH COLOUR AND SHADE

Shading techniques based on blending colour are an exciting stage in your make-up process, which can lift, and bring shine and sparkle to your whole appearance. Blushers are the key; the brighter shades as highlighter, the more subtle as a delicate form of contouring. Our African ancestors used vegetable dye to stain their cheeks.

BLUSHERS

- *Powder type. This is the one easily obtainable in Africa, since the heat does not affect its shelf life, as it does the other types. It usually comes with its own applicator, and is good for oily skin. Use over powder, or when moisturiser and foundation have settled, if you don't wear powder.*
- *Cream type. In compacts, sticks or*

Blusher blended over the cheekbones brightens up skin-tones.

pencils. Good for dry skin, with a natural sheen.
- *Liquid or gel, again for dry skins. These are transparent colours to give a glossy look. They can streak and be hard to control, but experiment over foundation, and don't powder.*

How to use blusher

No make-up should be smeared or rubbed on, especially blusher. Dot it on with a clean finger tip or its own applicator, with a light, stippling touch like the painter you are. Blend and feather with your special brush, so there will be no harsh obvious lines. You can try shades of blusher in a dark earthy tone in the hollows of your cheeks, blended upwards and outwards towards the middle of your ears, to contour your face. Use a lighter and more brilliant one on your cheekbones, blended to taper towards your temples, but never into the hairline. Naturally these colours must blend evenly into each other, otherwise the line of demarcation will look like badly-done fake tribal marks!

Colours to blush in

The colours you choose will be according to your shade of black skin. Experiment by mixing them, until you find a suitable shade, but here are some suggestions:-
- *Ebony. With jet-black skin, try shades of wine, plum, purple and bronze. Darker skinned women look stunning in beautifully blended shades of red blusher and eyeshadow (like the singer Grace Jones.)*
- *Brown skin. With a medium to light brown skin, try corals, deep orange, russet and rose. Avoid browns which dull your skin and hardly show.*
- *Light skin. Pink, red and orange set you glowing.*

Our skin looks dazzling with all shades of metallic glints, such as gold, bronze or copper. Use as highlights in the evening: down the centre of the nose, the temples and under the outer corner of the eyebrows.

FACE POWDER

Powder adds the finishing touch, setting your make-up and removing excessive shine, without losing the natural glow of the skin. It comes in many colours and forms, but having gone to all that trouble to select the appropriate foundation shade, why not use transluscent powder, that highlights your base? Sparkling ones are great at night.

Types

- *Loose powder comes in a box, which can be messy to carry around, but frosted and metallic powders usually come in this form.*
- *Compressed powder in a compact with its own puff or brush is much easier to keep in your bag for touching-up.*

    Use powder in moderation, and mostly for your T-areas. Apply the smallest amount over the cheekbones (because you may be adding another layer on top – the blusher.) Avoiding your hairline, press transluscent powder all over your face and neck in order to set your make-up for the whole day. Don't use too much around the eyes, where it may settle into fine lines. Brush off the excess. Alternatively, a lasting make-up is achieved by pressing a cold, damp sponge over your whole face and neck, but don't smudge the artistry!

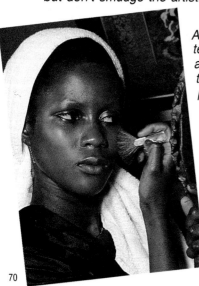

A model-girl technique is the application of translucent powder all over the face and neck, to give a glowing look.

EYES

These are the windows of your soul and of your health. They are the mirror of your personality and a reflection of your beauty. So take good care of them, both internally and externally. Those eyes are the first area to betray your age, and whether you smile or worry a lot, if you smoke, drink or suffer from a polluted environment. Rubbing and rough removal of make-up are but two of the constant agressions that eyes endure.

CARE FROM THE INSIDE

Eat food rich in Vitamin A (carrots and liver), essential for good eyesight, especially at night. The Vitamin B group ensures the health of the nerve supply to the eyes, and acts to ensure youthful skin in that area. B vitamins are found in liver, eggs, brown rice and wheatgerm. Vitamin C keeps the mucus linings of the eyes healthy, thus preventing infection; and is abundant in citrus fruits, tomatoes and green vegetables.

CARE FROM THE OUTSIDE

The skin around the eyes and especially under them is much thinner than anywhere else on the face, so don't pull or stretch it when applying or removing make-up. To remove small foreign bodies from the eyes, don't rub them or allow anyone to blow into your eyes, due to the risk of infection. Bathe your eyes with cooled, boiled water, containing some sea salt, or use eye-bathing lotion. But don't make too much of a habit of using commercial eye drops.

If your eyes look dull and tired, why not try a few early nights in a row? Read in adequate light coming from behind rather than from above, and avoid reading in a moving vehicle. Eyes really need rest and relaxation, just as you do, so after an hour, stop reading or typing for a few minutes.

Be sure to keep all your eye cosmetic applicators scrupulously clean, and never share them with anyone. Passing round the Kohl, in the traditional context, is still the fastest way of spreading conjunctivitis. Gazing directly at the sun also damages the eyes, so invest in a pair of good quality sunglasses.

Dark circles under the eyes or swelling around the eyes could be due to a lack of sleep, or to a kidney problem. Before resorting to home care, first consult your doctor. If nothing is seriously wrong, and your looks require instant resurrection, try applying iced water or milk on cotton pads. Another remedy is to lie down with a slice of cucumber placed over each closed eye for ten minutes, or place grated raw potatoes between two pieces of gauze on your lids.

EYE MAKE-UP

If you wear make-up on other parts of your face, you should balance it by colouring your eyes too. Black and Oriental women are reputed to have eyes that are striking in shape. African women have been aware of this fact, and over the centuries have applied their traditional eye cosmetics to stunning effect.

First examine the shape of your eyes and eyebrows. Are your eyes large, small, bulging or deep-set? There are lots of ways to use make-up to improve the shape of this – your most significant feature.

EYEBROWS

The next stage is to tidy up, re-shape and define your eyebrows, keeping them as natural as possible. Your eyebrows frame your eyes, balancing the features and nature has usually given you the shape to match your face. So don't try to change the shape too drastically. However, very bushy, straggly eyebrows are unfeminine, and cancel out the work you are going to do to your eyes. Because eyebrows also give the face its expression, the curve must not be over-exaggerated; so avoid high, thin arches that give your face an unatural permanently surprised look.

Eyebrow shape

Sit in front of a mirror and hold a pencil against your nose to form a line up to the inner corner

Feathery pencil strokes lift and extend the eyebrow arc.

of the eye, and then up to the eyebrow. Your eyebrow starts where the pencil touches it. Then hold the pencil diagonally from the base of your nose towards the ears, just past the outer corner of the eye. This is where your eyebrow ends, the highest point being directly above your iris.

If you prefer not to reshape your eyebrows, tidy them up regularly by brushing them into shape. Remove the stray ones between the brows and along the bottom of the eyebrows; never remove from above. If your eyebrows are a little wild, apply a little bit of petroleum jelly or moisturiser and brush into place.

Plucking your eyebrows

Cleanse your face and tie your hair back. Wash and dry your hands and disinfect the tweezers. Sitting before the mirror and in good light, brush your eyebrows into shape and work carefully from the lowest hair upwards. Hold the skin taut between your first and second fingers, remove only one hair (complete with root) at a time, plucking in the direction of hair growth. Your eyebrow should begin and end at the same level. When you have finished, wipe the eyebrows with a little toner, apply moisturiser and to avoid infection, don't use make-up immediately. Once a week check, and remove new growth.

Defining your eyebrows

You can use pencil or brush on powder, though pencils are more easily available in Africa. Black pencil is harsh and ageing, so use a shade lighter than your skin, like dark brown, mixed with charcoal grey. Strong lines are as peculiar looking as over-exaggerated arches.

Brush the eyebrows into shape, starting from the inner corner, and using a sharp pencil, make short, feathery strokes, following the direction of the hair growth. Shorten and slant the strokes softly downward at the outer end. Brush again for a natural look.

EYESHADOWS

Eyeshadow comes in matt, shiny or frosted form as pressed powder, a cream stick or liquid cream, of which the pressed powder is easiest to apply. Obviously, application varies with eye formation, so do some experimenting, to find the most flattering method. And don't remain wedded to that method for life; fashions in application change. Many women apply a pale base coat over the entire area of the eye socket, and then blending in a deeper tone, for example, on the lid. If you use two colours make sure they blend gently into each other. Always work from the inner side outwards, and don't apply too close to the nose.

An eyeshadow lighter than your basic colour is smoothed beneath the eyebrow, as a highlighter.

Complete the eye-shadowing in a creative way, choosing a colour to complement your clothes.

THE ARTIST AT WORK, COLOURING THE EYES

Before reaching for your palette and brush, let's consider suitable colours to put on it. Eye make-up should emphasise your eyes and show off their beauty and colour. The colours of eye shadows that best compliment our dark skins and brown-black eyes are dark browns, navy blue, dark green and purple. For highlights, try gold, bronze, beige, pale mauve, violet and dusty pink. Now you can have the fun of mixing these colours to your taste, working on the principle again that light colours bring out and emphasise an area, and dark colours deepen or make them recede.

Prominent or bulging eyes

If too prominent, first consult your doctor to make sure that you have nothing wrong with your thyroid gland. To create an illusion of recession, blend dark but not shiny eyeshadow in dark grey, greyish-black or very dark brown into the whole of the lower brow area, curving around the bottom corner of the eye. Use a dull softer highlight in bronze or beige, not a light or over-bright colour. With a dark brown pencil, draw a line along your crease line and smudge it. Use eyeliner to reduce the lid, but not to achieve a Cleopatra look.

Eyes too wide apart

With your eyebrow pencil, bring your brows closer together by lightly pencilling in some fake eyebrows nearer to your nose area. Use dark eyeshadow between the eyes and the bridge of the nose, blending upwards towards the brow line, then curving down to taper to the outer corner. Highlight a large deep part of the outside edge of the eye area, using colours that are not too pale, like mauve.

Eyes too close together

Here you want to create the opposite effect, by separating the eyes. The emphasis is on the outer part now. Pluck the space between the eyes near to the nose and with your pencil

extend the brow line out at the ends, curving naturally. Use a darker shade of eyeshadow and don't apply too close to the nose, beginning from the centre of the eye, blending outwards and upwards. Use a very light, bright highlight in gold or light yellow for the outer corner of the eye under the brow line.

Deep-set eyes

Raise them by pencilling in a few more false hairs a little above the natural brow line. Bring them out with lighter shades over the lid to just above the hollow. Use darker colour on the remaining outer corner of the eye, blending upwards. Apply highlight under the brow.

EYELINERS AND PENCILS

These define and emphasise the shape of the eyes, and if used cleverly, they open up the eyes, making the lashes appear thicker. There are:-

- *Liquid eyeliner, which is sometimes difficult to control, especially when you are in a hurry, and can look hard, though recently there has been a return to coloured eyeliners.*
- *Pencils come in many colours, including gold, and are easily obtainable.*

Paint on a narrow line of eyeliner from the inside corner of the eye, depending on the look you want. Grey and brown are good for defining (black is too harsh). If you prefer more colour, line the eyelid with dark blue, wine or purple, but avoid white or very light colours on eyelids. The contrast is too strong and unflattering on black skins. Why not try applying a different colour at the top and bottom of your eyes? Then

Use coloured or brown eye pencil or liner in thin lines along the upper lid and beneath the eye.

soften the lines slightly with a Q tip or slightly damp brush, blending into the eyeshadow.

MASCARA

Mascara can make the eyes look more glamorous and exotic by giving the appearance of thicker, longer, darker eyelashes. They are usually in liquid form in a tube with an applicator. Some contain fibres for added effect, but avoid these if you have sensitive eyes or wear contact lenses. Waterproof mascara is difficult to remove, without stretching the delicate skin around the eyes. If your eyes water at the slightest provocation, try hypo-allergenic mascaras.

For added eye drama, try using blue, green or purple mascara. But if your lashes are already long and thick, they may look too heavy with coats of mascara. Lightly apply some moisturiser or petroleum jelly, brushing the top lashes upwards and lower ones downwards with a clean mascara brush.

Applying mascara

Apply mascara on the tips of the eyelashes first, then to the top side of the upper lashes, brushing downwards from the base. Allow to dry, then brush mascara on from below, upwards. Brush lower lashes up first and then down. Brush to separate the lashes if they have stuck together. Allow to dry and repeat for a fuller effect.

To remove mascara, you can use special eye make-up removers, but corn oil, olive oil or baby oil do the job just as well. Apply with cotton wool to the whole eye area; leaving to dissolve the make-up for about thirty seconds. Wipe each eye gently from the inner corner outwards, with a cotton wool swab until clean. Wipe upper and lower lashes separately, to remove all traces of mascara.

SPECTACLES

Just because you need spectacles, doesn't mean that you should hide away behind them. In fact the full battery of eye make-up techniques should be intensified in your case.

Upper and lower lashes are brushed with two light coats of black mascara.

Use heavier liner, shadow and mascara behind your lenses, and choose colours that not only complement your eye-colour and outfit, but also the spectacle frames too.

THE PERFECT MOUTH

The perfect mouth means soft, inviting lips that reveal sparkling white teeth, one of our greatest assets. Brush them at least twice a day, and visit your dentist regularly.

Black peoples' mouths and lips are prominent and very expressive. We can use this to the greatest advantage by shaping and colouring to give luscious, sensuous lips. But they need care; lips have no lubricating oil and are often the driest part of the body. Smoking, extremes of temperature and constant wetting with saliva all make them drier. Cream them at night, and when not wearing make-up, use baby oil, petroleum jelly or lip salve.

Lipstick adds the final touch to your make-up. Our sisters in the village are fully aware of its powerful effect, and some stain their lips with vegetable dyes, even if they don't wear any other traditional make-up.

Some lipsticks give good lip coverage, others are intended to add a thin coloured gloss. Thin lip pencils are for outlining, thicker ones for filling in. First examine your unpainted lips in daylight, taking note of their shape, fullness and colour. Black women often have darker lips than their complexion, or their lower lip lighter than the upper one. The use of colours can correct this.

CHOOSING THE RIGHT COLOURS

Your skin colour determines your choice, and there should not be too much contrast with the colour of your face. Therefore dark women look strange in pale pinks, white-based or fluorescent bright colours that stand out like a beacon on our skin. The best colours to choose are:-

- *Browns, warm tones with a touch of copper, bronze, coral or paprika. Flat earthy tones are dull.*
- *Burgundies and dark reds.*
- *Mauves, but neither too dark nor too bright.*
- *Deep corals, terracotta or laterite colours.*

If you have difficulty in getting the right shades, blend the colours until you get what you want. Mix in tinted lip gloss to tone down bright red lipstick, or apply dark foundation to your lips first.

A chemical reaction between the skin and lip colours may change the actual colour of the lipstick on you. So always test on the part of your wrist closest to the colour of your lips, and allow time for this reaction before deciding (in daylight.) Remember you will need a darker more intense lipstick under electricity. The colour you choose should go with your eye colours, nail colour, blusher and of course your outfit. Also balance eyes and lip colours, so that one or the other dominates your appearance in brilliance. If both are strong or over-subtle, your face looks flat, with no contrast to create interest.

OUTLINING

Outlining with a lip pencil to define the normal shape of lips ensures superb results. It frames the lips to the best advantage, giving a neater look. But outlining to reshape thick or thin lips, like over-contouring of the face, always looks obvious. Be proud of your lips. If you consider them too full, use dark natural tones and don't apply too much.

With a magnifying mirror, using a thin, sharp lip pencil or fine lip brush in a shade darker but close to your lipstick colour, outline the lips. Work from the centre towards the corners for the top lip and from side to side for the lower lip.

Stroke your lip brush on the lipstick to gather some colour and fill in the lips evenly in the same movements as for the lip liner. If you wish, follow with lip gloss. Blotting can remove too much colour, dulling your make-up. The appeal of lips is heightened by a suggestion of wetness or sheen.

Outline your lips with a lip brush or a lip pencil a shade darker and toning with your lipstick.

For the final razzle-dazzle, dust a light layer of gold glitter powder over your face, neck and shoulders.

MATCHING CLOTHES AND MAKE-UP

It may sometimes be difficult to precisely match colours, clothes and make-up, so aim at toning rather than actual matching. Orange does not go with reds very well, but bronze and terracotta tone well with brown and beige outfits.

The main guideline is to wear clearly defined colours of lipstick with clothes in one strong colour, like black, dark grey or navy blue. With softer, paler colours like white, beige or pastels, wear lipstick in more subtle colours. Some African cloths are very colourful, especially the printed ones. Tone down your entire make-up in colour and intensity. Too many strong colours will be overpowering. If you are wearing a brilliant print, harmonise your make-up colours around one quiet colour in the fabric.

BEAUTY IN MATURITY

Age comes to us all, but it is possible to grow old elegantly and with dignity. Many signs of ageing are inherited, so the faces of your parents will give you an idea of how you will look in later years. The appearance of slowing down the clock is possible with effective skin-care and appropriate, flattering make-up. Lines and then wrinkles form on your face according to your habitual expressions, but there is also a decrease of elasticity in your skin, that vital collagen; a shrinking of the tissues beneath the skin; and hormonal changes.

Although black skin is reputed to be oilier and slower to age than white skin, the oiliness does decrease with age. So as you begin to notice lines developing, decrease the frequency with which you wash your face, and increase the amount of rich moisturiser you lavish in. Obviously those normal enemies of glowing skin are now your arch-enemies, like smoking, an abuse of alchohol, too much sun and central heating or air conditioning, and improper cleansing.

It is possible to grow old elegantly.

Moisturiser should be your constant friend, especially around your eyes, the area which ages first. Using your ring finger, to avoid stretching the skin, gently massage in coconut oil or wheatgerm oil. In fact you can carry on all over your body, not forgetting your neck, another area which goes 'crèpey' quickly.

Unconsciously, you will have been adjusting your make-up, so that it is appropriate to the dignity of your years, rather than to a disco-swinger! Remember that a mask-like effect, designed to hide unwanted signs, will not only look more ageing, but it can block up your pores. Aim for a transluscent semi-matt complexion, but avoid using too much powder, which can settle nastily in lines. Your blusher and lipstick look more flattering in warm tones of burgundy, plum and dark red. Keep your lips very well moisturised when not wearing lipstick.

There are of course drastic methods of trying to stay looking young, which give the effect of an over eager attempt to do just that. Last-ditch attempts such as face-lifts and silicone treatment are not the actions of a woman who believes in herself. Slightly less expensive are hormone creams, but effective deep skin care and attention to diet and exercise – yes, *especially* at your age, married to an acceptance of yourself in all the glorious achievement of maturity – this is the recipe for being a truly beautiful old lady.

THE WELL FINISHED LOOK

When you have completed your make-up stand back at least a metre away from your mirror, and assess the final effect, making changes if necessary. Never be half-hearted in your approach to make-up. If you wear it, it should be definite, meticulously applied and balanced. There is nothing more dating than wearing the same make-up year in, year out. Let your make-up move with the fashion, but use only the colours and products you feel right and confident in. When you are visiting in the countryside, tone the whole thing down. Why

not leave it off completely, cleanse and moisturise your face, and let your skin enjoy the clean, country air?

CARE OF HANDS AND NAILS

The great detective 'Sherlock Holmes' held that a person's hands are the first area to reveal their occupation and age. But take heart, with regular loving care, you can slow down the passage of time and conceal from the world that you, rather than a maid, do the manual labour around the house.

At the risk of sounding repetitive, it must be emphasised how important diet is to the condition of the skin stretched in such a tell-tale way across your hands. And at the risk of being boring, moisture is the key. Moisturise your hands at any given opportunity, keeping some good rich handcream, possibly containing glycerine as a barrier, beside your bathroom hand-basin, bed and kitchen sink. If it *is* you washing the clothes and dishes, why not wear rubber gloves to protect your hands from all the harmful chemicals involved in housework? Go as far as to wear gardening gloves, as contact with the soil seems to be very drying too.

As you get older, specific exercise of the hands is no bad idea, even if you think they are quite active enough. Arthritis is not amusing. Try placing a tennis ball in your hand, squeezing and relaxing alternately. To exercise your fingers, imagine you are playing a piano. Stretch out your fingers, moving them up and down rapidly on the keys. Ward off arthritis or rheumatism by practising these daily a few times.

FINGERNAILS

Though it is tempting, please don't use them as tools, if you don't want them to break. Obviously, if you bite your nails, you can't expect to have long, elegant ones.

Take a good look at your nails. Are they brittle or peeling? Are the cuticles (at the base of the nail) damaged? That is, are they split, puffy or sore? Apart from exposure to damaging chemicals, these problems could be due to ill-health, or even to careless manicuring. The use of varnish-remover without washing your nails thoroughly afterwards, is really asking for trouble. Imagine if it can take off four coats from your nails, what else is it doing to them?

THE MANICURE

Allow at least half an hour for this, and consider it a luxurious process of self care. Give yourself a home manicure once or twice a month, and the real treat of the professional service every few months. Avoid applying new polish more than once a week; expert application should ensure that it lasts up to four days, perhaps with the help of a little touching-up at the tips. Then let your nails breathe for a few days; otherwise acetone-based chemicals can damage your nails.

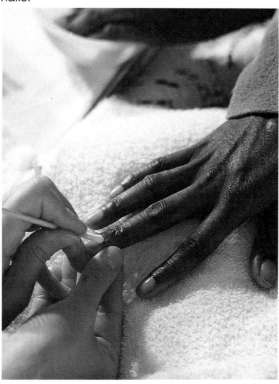

The technique

- *Remove old nail varnish and wash your hands very thoroughly.*
- *To loosen any dirt under the tips, rather than poking around with sharp instruments, soak your fingers in a bowl of warm water to which a slice of lemon has been added. If your nails are brittle or peeling, add a little olive oil.*
- *Massage special cuticle cream into that area and the surrounding nail.*
- *Push the cuticles back very gently, using the smooth rubber end of an 'orange' stick, designed for the job. Never ever use a sharp object, as this is the bedrock of future nail growth.*
- *File rather than cut finger nails, for greater control in shaping, from the sides to the centre; never saw. Use an emery board, rather than a metal file, as the latter can jar the new nail growth. File to an oval or rounded shape, rather than pointed witches' claws, which not only look old-fashioned, but can weaken the nail structure and growth pattern. Smooth off the filed surface with the back of the emery board, working away from yourself.*
- *Resoak your hands for five minutes in the same therapeutic liquid as above, and dry well.*
- *If you use nail varnish, begin with a specially formulated base coat, to prevent absorption of the colour pigments to follow, and to provide a smooth foundation, if you have ridged nails. Apply two thin coats of nail varnish, allowing each coat to dry well, before adding another.*
- *To ensure a lasting varnish and to add a glossy finish, apply a special top coat, which is clear.*

Massage the cuticles with cuticle cream, and gently nudge them back with an orange stick or Q-tip.

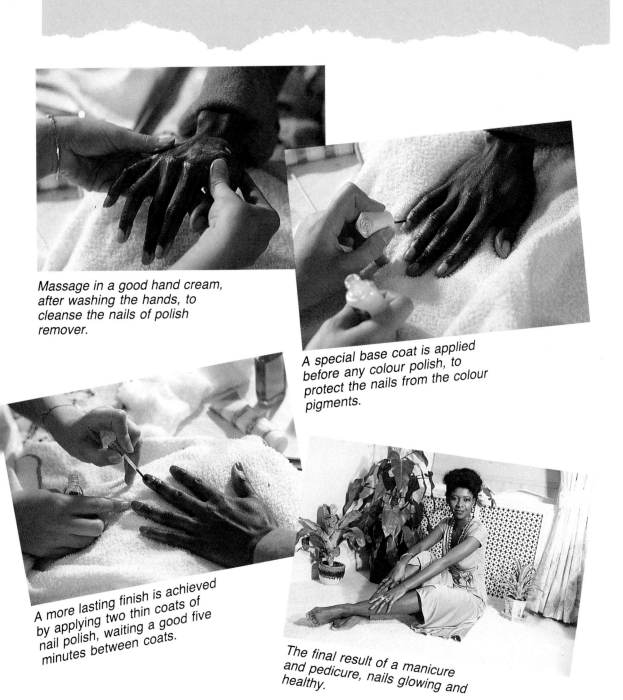

Massage in a good hand cream, after washing the hands, to cleanse the nails of polish remover.

A special base coat is applied before any colour polish, to protect the nails from the colour pigments.

A more lasting finish is achieved by applying two thin coats of nail polish, waiting a good five minutes between coats.

The final result of a manicure and pedicure, nails glowing and healthy.

FOOT CARE

Our feet are certainly one of the most abused parts of our bodies. Thank goodness they let us know when they've had enough.

The correct shape and size of shoes is vital. Your shoes must fit perfectly, especially around the heels, and allow plenty of room for you to wriggle your toes. They must not pinch, rub or squeeze any part of your foot, and don't expect the shoe to stretch later; your feet will suffer before it does. Good arch support is also important.

Comfort really is as important as fashion, though fortunately the trend for flatter shoes seems here to stay, in tune with our fast-moving life styles. Very pointed shoes and other extremes of fashion can cause bunions, (especially to growing teenage feet) or corns. If you have developed a corn, do not try to remove it yourself with a razor blade, as this can cause severe bleeding and infection. Wear corn pads or have them surgically removed by a chiropodist. Bunions too can be soothed with a bunion pad, worn inside the shoe or professionally removed, though this type of surgery is a very risky and drastic step.

Observe rigorous foot hygiene. You can rub a pumice stone over your heels, to gradually remove dead, hard skin. Dry your feet very thoroughly, especially in between the toes, to avoid cracking. Rub your feet, especially the soles with body lotion or hand cream. Get someone who loves you to give you a soothing foot massage once a week!

THE PEDICURE

Also to be lovingly applied once a week!
- *Just as for your manicure, first remove all traces of polish and wash thoroughly.*
- *Trim your toe nails with nail scissors or a special toe nail clipper, cutting the nails straight across.*
- *Apply petroleum jelly generously to the base and sides of the nails with your fingertips, and soak both feet in warm soapy water, for about ten minutes.*
- *Brush the nails and cuticles with a nail brush (kept specially for this purpose) and dry well.*
- *Gently ease back the cuticles using your orange stick.*
- *Rub moisturiser all over your feet.*
- *If you use varnish, apply as for the manicure.*

Give your feet a rest by going bare-foot around the house. After a tiring day, soak them for fifteen minutes in lukewarm water to which a slice of lemon has been added. Rinse in cool water and moisturise. Lie down and elevate the feet on a cushion, to reduce congestion in the legs and feet.

An excellent relaxing foot exercise, particularly if you are pregnant, is to rotate each foot at the ankle, first in a clockwise, then in an anti-clockwise direction, each for about thirty seconds. Pamper your feet and they will serve you well.

THE ARTIST'S FINISHING TOUCH

Africans love gold, as a hair decoration, as jewellery around the neck, wrists, fingers, ankles; as amulets when in traditional costume, and as gold threads in the weave of our cloth. Black skin and gold, brown skin and gold, are rich and exotic. For evening, dot gold powder at the top centre of the upper lip, use a touch of gold highlighter on the lower lip, or try gold-tinted nail varnish. If wearing a low-cut dress or wrapper-style traditional costume without the Buba, dust your collar bone lightly with gold powder or highlighter. It all adds to your style as a Black beautiful woman.

CHAPTER 7

HAIR AS LIVING SCULPTURE

'Beautiful is the hair over the ears, a matter of pride' – Song of the Bega women hairdressers of East Africa.

Hair may be a woman's crowning glory, but in Black societies, especially in Africa, it is much more than that. Padded, extended and supported in an amazing variety of forms, it is styled, glistening with oil, packed with mud or clay, and elaborately decorated to reflect a woman's culture, status or different stages and events in her life. The dramatic, intricate and beautiful coiffures are architectural triumphs, and reflect not only the hairdressers' artistic talents, but also an inborn sense of geometry.

For those wanting a change from the traditional, the versatility of our hair has no limitations; its texture lends itself to endless creative variation. Imitations of our hairstyles by the Western world, like the Bo Derek plaits, is the sincerest form of flattery. In most African societies, the head is the seat of spiritual power; hence the proportionally larger heads of African sculpture, and the concentration on hairstyles as a focus of adornment. The competition in hairdressing between the sexes is often fierce in some parts of Africa, such as the Nubians of Sudan, but women usually excell all over the continent. So what is this apparently lifeless material that can crown the head of a sophisticated Mali princess, bring work to a top international model, or plunge us into despair?

THE STRUCTURE OF HAIR

To understand and appreciate the importance of proper hair care, you need some basic information on its consistency, growth and functions, and how to cope when things go wrong.

Each hair on your head is dead, just like your fingernails! Only the follicle in which the birth, growth and death of each hair occurs, is alive. The follicle is a little bulb under the skin. At the base is a clump of cells called the 'papilla' that produce the keratin cells, which become a strand of hair. Keratin is a protein rich in sulphur and resistant to acids. Alkaline agents however can damage the hair.

When a hair is plucked out, the papilla is left behind and makes a replacement, hence your plucked eyebrows soon need re-plucking. The papilla is richly supplied with tiny blood vessels that nourish it with food and oxygen and remove its waste products. The follicle also contains an oil gland, which supplies the natural oil flowing along a wick to coat each hair and protect it from water loss. This affects the dryness or oiliness of your hair.

Hair is an extension of the skin, and has three layers. The first or outer layer, the 'cuticle', consists of overlapping layers of cells like fish scales, that normally lie flat and smooth against the hair shaft, and guard against excessive evaporation of water. The cuticle provides about 35% of your hair's desirable elastic strength. Underneath is the threadlike 'cortex' containing the colour-bearing melanin, and composed of keratin. It is the thickest part of the hair, softer than the cuticle, yet providing about 65% of the hairs' elastic strength.

Chemical changes like colouring and relaxing have to reach the cortex to be effective; and improper use or overprocessing, can cause damage, resulting in dry, weak and brittle hair with split ends.

The innermost layer is the 'medulla', largely made up of air spaces with fragments of melanin and soft keratin. The medulla is often absent, but this does not affect the condition of the hair.

HAIR IN ACTION

Anagen, Catagen and Telogen (ACT) are the three stages of hair growth, which with some hair loss, are a constant normal process. It is worth understanding this growth pattern to avoid unnecessary worry on seeing hairs on your brush or comb. An individual hair grows from two to five years in the Anagen period, during which growth is faster in hot weather or in exposure to sunlight. There is slower growth at night and in very cold weather.

Then comes the degenerative, transitional phase, Catagen, lasting only a few weeks, in which the hair follicle stops growing and shrinks, and the papilla stops producing. It then enters the resting or Telogen phase, when its root weakens and it is either brushed, combed or pushed out by a new growing hair. This lasts about three to six months, after which it's back to the Anagen or active growth phase, as long as the follicle is alive and healthy. If the follicle is dead, no new hair grows and permanent baldness occurs, depending on the number affected. However, about 85% of your hairs are in the Anagen phase, the rest being in either the Catagen or Telogen phase at any one time. So keep your hair on, and don't panic about hair loss.

HAIR AND RACE

Although the hair of Black people is usually curly, not all of our hair has the same curls or wave patterns, and like the many shades of our black skin, the combinations and variations of curls and waves make our hair both unique and dynamic.

A young Moroccan girl with plaits and beads.

Cascading curls of a Guyanese woman.

Classical 'African' – type hair of a woman from Sierra Leone.

The curliness or straightness of hair is determined by heredity, racial characteristics being a very strong factor. Our hair is generally very porous, a bit coarse (which lends itself to all those styling possibilities), with much natural body and strong wave patterns. But it is very delicate and can break easily. If you are wearing your hair 'natural', pull out one strand, and place it on a white background. You will see that apart from looking like a corkscrew, the strand is thick in some places and thin in others, twisting wherever it forms a curl – the twists are the most fragile part and the cause of those tangles. So always comb gently and whether relaxed or natural, remember: 'Fragile, handle with care.'

A KALEIDOSCOPE OF COLOURS, TYPES, SHAPES AND LENGTHS

Women across the Black Diaspora may have hair which varies from cascading curly blond, to thick, woolly, black hair. In Africa too, black hair varies considerably in length, curliness, frizziness, shine and so on. The important thing to know is what type of hair you have, as this will help you to decide on the appropriate care and style. But remember that the thickness, colour, curliness, length, oiliness or dryness depend on what you inherited from your parents, while the condition is largely up to you. So work with what you have rather than fighting it, or making too drastic a change and damaging your hair. So what type are you?

THICK OR THIN

Hair may be normal, with a faint coating of sebum, smooth-surfaced whether wet or dry and elastic. The scalp is free of dandruff and slightly oily. It has a healthy and attractive appearance, and is of the right texture and density. The lack of shine is normal, since black hair, because of its corkscrew shape, does not reflect the light in the same way as straight hair. Hair may be fine to the touch, but not necessarily thin, (meaning only a few hairs per square inch). So it is possible to have a head of fine hair that is abundantly thick, or coarse hair that is very scanty, although it may look thicker.

If your hair is both fine and thin, nothing will make it thicker. Accept this and give it tender loving care. Use a very mild shampoo and a rich, penetrating conditioner to give it body. You can also try those setting mousses for extra body. Never straighten with a hot comb, but use the mildest relaxers if you want to straighten it. Try small rollers to make it look thicker. Individual plaits with extensions also give it body, but the plaits should be fairly loose, to avoid pulling out what little you've got!

Thick hair is the envy of us all, particulary if it is long. Although it is less of a problem, the washing, grooming and styling may sometimes be difficult. It also needs tender loving care. Never comb or brush in a hurry, and first separate the tangles gently with your fingers. If you want straightened hair, thick hair can take all processes well, but with the usual precautions.

Thick hair can also look fantastic in plaits, corn row or threaded. In some parts of Africa, frequent head-aches are often associated with thick long hair, and out come the scissors as a drastic cure! If you are blessed with this type of hair, treasure it, and first consult your doctor before getting the chop. Your head-aches may be due to high blood pressure, an eye defect or even to malaria!

LONG OR SHORT

The length of black womens' hair varies considerably. While the intermingling of races has caused some of us to have long hair that falls down our backs like Caucasian hair, I have seen many black women in Africa, with negroid hair that reaches beyond the shoulders, when threaded or plaited.

There are black women all over the world whose hair will just not grow. They don't use chemicals on their hair, it appears healthy, but will not grow. This condition is hereditary, so accept it, but avoid having your hair done in tight braids or threading, in the hope that this will lengthen the hair. It could lead to hair loss. Consider the use of extensions or simply wear your hair natural in a short, sculpted Afro.

HAIR COLOUR

Our hair, like our skin, is a kaleidoscope of colours, ranging from a sandy blonde to jet black, and including all shades of brown and auburn. Generally speaking, most of us have black or off-black, or dark brown hair. There is a definite link between the pigmentation of our skin and how it conforms with skin and eye colour. We shall discuss suitable colour changes under Colouring.

HAIR HEALTH AND BEAUTY

INTERNAL FACTORS

A beautiful healthy head of hair is often a source of envy or admiration, depending on the state yours is in! The health of your hair depends on the internal state of your body. Hair depends on the blood running underneath its surface for its nourishment, just like any other part of the body. Inadequate knowledge of the effect of our mental and physical health on hair, and the endless damage self-inflicted in the interests of fashion, have caused many unnecessary hair problems.

The hair, like the face, is a good indicator of your state of mind. Sudden emotional shock or stress can throw the growing hairs out of phase with one another, so that they reach the end of their growing phase at the same time, falling out simultaneously. The condition can be reversed, if you try and solve your problems in time, so never despair. If your hair looks awful, the chances are that you will not be feeling lively, when you look in the mirror.

A common culprit of hair that is out of condition is birth control pills. Consider changing to another form of birth control, if your hair is causing concern. Taking the Pill again after childbirth can also affect your hair health. Tranquilisers, thyroid pills and aspirin are all potential hair hazards.

As we have seen, you are what you eat, and this applies to your hair as much as it does to any other part of your body. Hair thrives best on foods rich in iron, zinc, and the hair 'beauty mineral' – sulphur. The Vitamin B complex group also boosts hair and scalp health. Hair is about 90% protein, so a regular and adequate variety of proteins affect its growth and cortex condition.

EXTERNAL FACTORS

Our hair may be our natural protection against the sun's rays, but not without suffering damage. The sun dries the hair and discolours it, so protect your hair with a hat or head-tie, whenever you have to be in the sun. You will also be protecting it from dust and other harmful air-pollutants, as well as warding off heat-stroke. The low humidity of an African winter also dries your hair. You may need a richer conditioner and to apply more oil than usual. In cold climates, central heating dries out your hair and skin. Excessive heat from blow-drying with a hair-dryer, over-processing with chemicals and dyes, the use of harsh bath soaps instead of shampoo for washing your hair, can all cause serious damage.

Swimming is a splendid form of exercise, but remember that the chlorine in swimming pools and the salt in sea water can ruin your hair. Apply a little oil or conditioning cream before you swim, and either wear a well-fitting cap or wash thoroughly immediately afterwards, and re-condition. Swimming with your hair in corn rows or plaits makes it difficult to completely remove the harmful substances, when you wash it.

IS YOUR HAIR HEALTHY?

Examine it thoroughly before you wash it next time. Pick up a strand of hair and run it through your fingers. Does it feel rough or smooth, especially at the ends? Roughness is a sign of dryness and damage. Now examine a few strands for 'porosity.' – Each hair naturally contains water; how much it can hold and how quickly it can absorb water determines the porosity. Pour a little water on yours. Does the water bounce off or is it quickly absorbed?

The degree of porosity of your hair depends on the state of the cuticle (outer layer). If the water is absorbed quickly, the cuticle is

damaged, causing the hair to lose its natural moisture. Another factor can be a lack of sebum to prevent evaporation of moisture, also causing the hair to dry out.

Now check the elasticity. Wet hair is like elastic, so take a strand and gradually pull. Healthy hair can stretch up to one third beyond its natural length, and then shrink back to normal, without any harm done.

HAIR PROBLEMS

DRY HAIR

This condition in black hair literally feels dry and wiry and the hair can be difficult to manage. The dry type of dandruff may also be a problem. First check if you are responsible for the damage done to your hair, before blaming nature. The oiliness of our hair depends first on the amount of oil produced, and its

distribution along the shaft to reach the ends. Hair constantly worn in the various traditional African styles, which include winding black thread tightly round the hair in small sections, can result in a condition in which the natural oils of the scalp cannot reach the ends of our hair. This is one of the reasons why we tend to oil our hair, when traditionally styled.

Once a week you can apply the tiniest amount of oil to your hair. Divide it into small sections, and bring the oil slowly up to the ends of the hair. This gives it some sheen and protects the delicate cortex. Apply a little to the scalp as well and massage in, to improve circulation. Ultra Sheen also gives the desired effect, along with other preparations, to suit individual hair preferences.

In Africa, local plants yield oils and fats as a base for pomades. Mixed with henna or indigo, they give a tint and gloss to the hair. Here are some popular ones used by our African sisters, all of which can be recommended, when used in small amounts:-

- *Groundnut oil.*
- *Palm kernel oil (good for the skin too).*
- *Beniseed oil.*
- *Oil of the wild olive (or spiny plum).*
- *Oil of the mahogany tree (Africolania elaesperma) is claimed to stimulate hair growth.*
- *Oil of the seeds of colocynth (colocythis vulgaris) is said to be effective for blackening grey hair.*

Care of dry hair

Remember that it is delicate and can break easily, so handle gently! Shampoo once every ten days, using a specially formulated shampoo. Before you start, give yourself an oil conditioning treatment. Wear a thin cotton scarf or hair net, protect your pillow and leave overnight, shampooing the following morning. More conditioning treatments for dry hair are discussed later.

Use your hair drier at a low setting, and don't blow dry more than once a week. Why not let your hair dry naturally, after patting with a towel? If you straighten, avoid over-hot combs and don't apply too much oil – you don't want to fry your hair. Use only oil-based laquers or hair sprays, and in moderation.

Split ends

These usually accompany dry or damaged hair, though oily hair too can develop split ends. In most cases the causes are self-inflicted by harsh processing, too much sun, the wrong method of shampooing, and rough handling, like combing or brushing vigorously when wet or while still warm, thereby splitting open the cuticle at the end of the hair. Once a month examine your hair for split ends or get a friend or your hairdresser to help. The remedy is the same as for dry hair. In addition, the split ends should be cut off, otherwise they will travel up the hair, causing breakage at several points.

OILY HAIR

If you are not applying too much oil and you notice an increase in oiliness a few days after washing it, then your hair is oily, due to over-production of oil by the sebaceous glands in your scalp. This may be accompanied by spots on the forehead and oily dandruff, and the hair will be difficult to manage. It is usually hereditary, but rich oily foods, nervous upsets or pregnancy can also cause the condition.

The remedy

Wash your hair weekly, using an acid-balanced shampoo and fairly hot water to remove the excess oil. You probably don't need a conditioner, unless you have relaxed or permanently coloured your hair, but use a lemon or vinegar rinse (see under Shampoo), which will further gently remove excess oil. Oily hair can tolerate processing better than dry hair, though your hair will look healthy and beautiful in a plaited style.

DANDRUFF

This is a problem of the scalp. The scalp skin is continuously shed unnoticed from the surface, and replaced by new skin from underneath, just like skin elsewhere on the body. But when the shedding becomes excessive and noticeable, it is called dandruff, which as we have seen can be of the dry or oily type. Dry dandruff makes the scalp rather itchy and shows up embarassingly on black hair as white powdery flakes. It may be due to poor health, a dry skin condition, or a Vitamin B12 deficiency.

Before you use any of the anti-dandruff shampoos, first apply the remedies for dry hair. If there is no improvement, try a mild anti-dandruff shampoo, but avoid harsh medicated ones, which can cause more dryness, and don't use these special shampoos all the time.

Oily dandruff is associated with oily skin. The shed skin cells clump together forming large flakes, due to the excess oil, and the scalp can be quite itchy and sore. A mild case should be treated in the same way as for oily hair. Medicated anti-dandruff shampoo should clear the condition, but again don't use this type of shampoo continuously, to avoid more hair damage. A severe case is called 'seborrhoeic dermatitis', with a rash spreading down the forehead, behind the ears, the eyebrows and even the eyelashes. This needs medical help.

HAIR LOSS – OR ALOPAECIA

The scalp is an indicator of our internal state, and we should always heed its warning signs. Hair can be lost suddenly or gradually over the years. Gradual loss makes it difficult to decide whether it is age, or causes like anaemia, due to lack of iron, a Vitamin B deficiency, a thyroid problem or a sudden shock. Medication with steroids such as hydrocortizone, inflammatory conditions and treatments for cancer such as radiotherapy and chemotherapy, high fevers or even childbirth, can all upset the phases of the growing hairs, making them fall out at the same time. So bear these causes in mind if you are losing your hair. Hair loss is more serious if sudden and can be caused by undiagnosed cancer or syphilis.

A popular belief in parts of Africa holds that hair loss in pregnancy means a female child. If the hair loss is excessive, the baby is adding the mother's hair to hers, and she will have beautiful long hair when she grows up! Such is the (erroneous) traditional belief in my part of

Nigeria, amongst the Yorubas of the west. During one of my pregnancies, I lost handfulls of hair, which was attributed to this cause. It was indeed a girl, and now she has grown up, she does have lovely long hair. But little did my family know that my hair loss was due to the necessary X-ray investigation I had in the seventh month of pregnancy, for a gall bladder condition!

A common self-inflicted hair loss among Blacks is traction alopaecia. Thank goodness it is temporary. In Africa, quite a large number of women have this condition, especially in those parts where the traditional styles are achieved by tying with thread. It simply pulls the hair out by the roots. We even inflict this punishment on our daughters at a very early age, in the hope that they will develop long luxurious hair. Other causes of traction alopaecia are any hairstyle that constantly pulls the hair at the roots, such as a tight pony tail, the use of tight rollers or elastic bands.

If you feel that your femininity is threatened, because you have suffered permanent hair loss, there are effective cosmetic remedies, such as 'weave on' and hair transplantation, though both can be expensive. Hair weaving is discussed under Style. Hair transplantation is uncommon in Africa. This may be because there are various traditional hairstyles which camouflage the hair loss, or the affected women simply wear a headtie or wig, most of the time.

Hair transplantation is scalp surgery in which small clumps of hair-bearing skin are taken from another part of the head with good healthy hair growth, and placed in 'punched-out' sites in the bald area. It is done in stages, with many visits to the trichologist, over a period of months or even years being necessary to complete the treatment. Beware of inexperienced or unqualified operators, if you are considering a transplant. If done properly, the success rate is quite high.

GREY HAIR

As we get older, the greying of the hair is a normal, progressive, physiological change and constitutes a slow fading of hair colour, rather than a sudden dramatic one. It is possible to turn grey overnight as a result of severe sudden shock or a high degree of mental strain and stress. Premature greyness is hereditary, sometimes only as a patch of grey. In Africa a prematurely grey girl is often believed to be the re-incarnation of her grand-mother, and she is treated with great respect.

Hair colour is determined by the amount and type (or colour) of the melanin pigment in the cortex or centre of each hair. Transparency of the cuticle (outside layer) allows the colour to shine through. As we get older, the melanin-producing cells are not as active. With no more colour pigments, the affected hairs become colourless or white and air bubbles replace the pigments. Once it has gone, you can't restore the colour, but cheer up, you can be even more elegant with your greying hair. It is a mark of dignity and distinction for a Black woman. But it should be well cared for and beautifully styled to suit your age. Camouflaging your grey hair is discussed under Colouring.

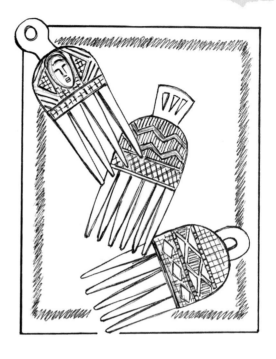

CARING FOR YOUR GREY HAIR

Grey hair is more delicate than black. If you decide to dye your hair, you should condition it at least twice a month, because the dye can make your hair brittle. Use a mild shampoo, and avoid too much heat from the sun or hot straightening combs, which can turn the grey hairs an ugly yellow or red. Use a mild relaxer if you want, and wear your hair either long or short. There is no reason why a mature woman should not wear her hair long; in Africa, long hair is a treasured asset.

THE BASIC TOOLS FOR HAIR-GROOMING

African combs are beautifully carved and decorated, and are mostly of wood or ivory, horn or tortoise shell. The types of combs and brushes you use depend upon your type of hair, and the style in which you wear it. Combs should have smooth rounded teeth to avoid scalp and hair damage. Wooden ones splinter,

cause hair to break, and are unhygenic. Unfortunately, they are the type most commonly used by African hairdressers. Never allow them near your hair. Take along your own natural or plastic ones. Have combs with varying teeth spacing, wide-toothed for wet or tangled hair, and less wide for styling. A good handle is important.

A comb is usually used for traditional African styles or tight curly hair. But for relaxed and other chemically straightened or curled hair, a good brush is also essential. The best for our hair have firm, round and well-spaced bristles, which should preferably be natural rather than plastic. A natural bristle hairbrush is a good investment – it won't tear your hair out! Always test a brush on your skin. If it pricks, don't use it. Gently comb wet hair, don't brush it, starting with your fingers if you like, if yours has a tendency to tangle.

In some parts of Africa, you may not have a good selection of hair brushes, so buy one or two the next time you travel to where they are available. Good hygiene is a law that must never be broken in hair grooming. Wash your combs and brushes more often than you wash your hair; you can even disinfect them in diluted antiseptic.

HAIR CARE

In skin care, we cleanse, tone and moisturise. Caring for our hair is really no different' for we shampoo, massage and condition it. You may be able to do a quickie cleansing and make-up routine, but in hair care, never be in a hurry. Handle with care, and you will reap the benefits.

SHAMPOOS

The purpose of a shampoo is to remove dirt, grease and dead scalp cells efficiently. It should be easily rinsed off and not dry the hair by damaging the cuticle and stripping it of its moisture.

Which shampoo?

The term 'PH' balanced which you may see on labels of some shampoos, refers to the chemical make up of hair products, of which some are acid, while others are alkaline. This property is measured on a scale of 1–14. Taking the number 7 as neutral, anything below 7 is acid, while any above 7 is alkaline.

The skin, hair and scalp have a PH of between 4 and 6, due to their slightly acid natural state as a means of fighting infection. This slightly acidic state must be maintained for healthy and manageable hair. Cake soap for bathing and detergents are highly alkaline and will damage the hair.

In Africa traditional shampoos vary considerably and they really cannot yet be recommended, because not enough research has been done, to ascertain their chemical properties. They include the juice of various plants containing saponis, such as the Resurrection plant (Bryophyllum pimmatum). Cloves crushed in water are also used. Commercial shampoos come as liquid, cream or gel, and are formulated for dry, normal or oily hair. Choose accordingly.

Washing your hair should be a pleasurable activity. To obtain the full enjoyment from this process, first assemble everything you will need, so that you are not dashing about dripping:-

- *A small bowl and three large buckets of warm water, if you have no shower facilities.*
- *Shampoo.*
- *Conditioner.*
- *A towel.*
- *Comb and brush.*
- *An optional colour rinse.*

Gently massage the scalp to loosen the dirt, brush or comb to untangle, and wet your hair thoroughly with warm (but not too hot) water. Pour some shampoo onto your hair, and gently massage it into your scalp and hair, using the fleshy part of your finger tips. There may be only a little lather this time, but it will loosen the dirt and grease and soften the cuticle. Rinse off the shampoo.

Now you are ready for the second dose. Pour on a little more shampoo and spread evenly throughout the hair, using a light circular massage action. Remember it's hair, not clothes, that you are washing. Rinse thoroughly at least three or four times, until all traces of the shampoo are removed, otherwise your hair will be damaged. Follow with cold water to tone your scalp and close the pores. Your hair is clean when the water pours off clean, which may be after the second rinse.

Don't wash your hair every day, it can 'strip' your crowning glory; once a week or every ten days is quite adequate. Finish off, if you like, with a lemon or vinegar rinse to help restore the acid balance of the hair and form a protective coating. Simply mix one cup of fresh lemon juice (or vinegar) with a cup of cool water (not for a scalp with sores or cuts, as it will sting.) Pour onto the hair and gently work through it. Long hair will need double the quantity. Leave for three minutes and rinse off completely in cool water.

If you are not conditioning your hair, pat dry gently with a clean soft towel and don't rub, to avoid hair breakage. Let your hair dry naturally, if you can, especially where the tropical heat and breeze can act as a natural blow drier!

CONDITIONING

Thank heavens for the wonderful world of conditioners. We have inflicted all sorts of horrors on our hair over the years, and but for hair conditioners, many of us would have harsh straw-like hair or even be bald! A conditioner repairs damage by coating the hair with a protective film, which paints over the cracks in the cuticle, making it smooth and easier to comb. A penetrating type, usually protein, enters the cortex and reacts with the hairs' protein, giving it temporary body. Most conditioners contain proteins, oils or waxes, or all three combined. If your hair has been processed, you will need to condition it after each shampoo.

Try some of the natural conditioners, and observe the change in your hair after each treatment, so that you can discover your favourite, but vary them from time to time.

Hot oil magic

This is an old, well-tried recipe, very effective for dry, brittle or damaged hair. It is a pre-shampoo treatment.
- *Olive oil.*
- *Odourless castor oil.*
- *Coconut oil.*

Mix in equal parts and warm slightly to 55°C. Stand the container in hot water to maintain this temperature. Part your hair into small sections, apply to the partings, taking the oil up to the ends of the hair as well. Massage well into the hair and scalp. Wring out a clean towel in hot water and wrap around your head for about thirty minutes. Re-heat the towel every ten minutes. Then shampoo and make sure that you remove all the oil. After about two or three latherings, you can follow with your usual conditioning treatment.

Egg conditioner

Egg yolk, being protein, has been used as a conditioner in many cultures. Just break two eggs (no, not on your head, but into a bowl.) Remove the whites, beat the yolks and apply to your hair after shampooing and rinsing. Leave for twenty minutes and rinse well. As a pre-shampoo treatment, mix about 5 tablespoons of olive oil thoroughly with the egg yolks, apply to dry hair, cover with paper towels or napkins, and put on an old but clean cotton scarf or a shower-cap. Leave for two hours and then shampoo and rinse thoroughly. This is an excellent hair restorer.

Bone marrow conditioner

A messy but effective hair food. Make friends with your butcher, and you will get a supply of large bones regularly. Remove the marrow and mix with two tablespoons of olive oil. Warm the brew and apply to your scalp and hair. Massage in well, covering your head with a warm towel as in the hot oil treatment. Either smother yourself in perfume or keep to yourself, because this treatment smells! Shampoo well and rinse.

Avocado Pack

A recipe for soft, smooth hair. In fact, you can feed your body on avocado, from the inside out. Eat it, moisturise your skin with it, and paste it on your hair.

Mash two ripe avocado pears, add drops of warm olive oil (two tablespoons) as you mix. Wet the hair and massage the paste into it and your scalp. Pop on your shower cap and leave for two hours. Rinse in warm water. Then shampoo and rinse as usual.

MASSAGE

Massage can really improve the condition of your hair and scalp. It is both relaxing and stimulates the circulation to the papillae and hair follicles. But it must be performed properly and regularly. Using the fleshy part of your finger tips and thumbs, make circular movements, on the scalp. Make sure you move the scalp over the skull without pulling at your hair; oil the scalp a little, if it is dry. Do small sections at a time until the whole scalp is covered. If you feel a delightful tingling sensation on the scalp, it's working. Spend at least twenty minutes a day on scalp massage, and if done properly, you should soon see the results.

RADICAL HAIR CHANGE

All forms of hair processing, like straightening with chemical relaxers or hot combs, colouring, tinting or chemical curling, are going to change the structure and condition of your hair. It need not be for the worse, provided you are prepared to care for your hair properly, conditioning it regularly. In Africa, damage of the hair is not usually because of a particular product, but as a result of mishandling, carelessness and perhaps the use of fake products. So make sure your source of supply is safe, reliable and constant.

COLOURING

Colouring hair is not new to Black women. The best-known and ancient dye, Henna, from the Lawsonia plant, is indigenous to Africa and Asia. Indigo, from the leaves of Loncho carpus cyanescens, is also used to give highlights and gloss to our hair. Apart from these, local dyes are not generally to be recommended, since some of them can coarsen the hair.

For the contemporary Black woman, a remarkable range of products and colours exists to give temporary or permanent change. One aim may be to colour grey hair, another to enrich natural hair colour, or again as an unusual fashion accessory. Natural-type hair colours complement our rich skin tones, more radical change can completely alter your image. All of them will boost your ego, though you should perhaps think a minute before going permanently fuscia pink or bright orange – you will be living with it, until that head of hair grows out!

Before you colour, find out about the products and how they function. You may not be able to obtain as many varieties in Africa, as in London or New York, but if you travel to such places, buy enough to last a few months, and store in the fridge. Colouring agents come in powders, creams, gels, colour crayons, sprays or liquids, or as vegetable dyes. What really counts is whether they are temporary, semi-permanent or permanent colouring.

Hair coloured and conditioned with Henna.

IMPORTANT PRECAUTIONS

- *Keep all colouring agents away from the eyes and out of the reach of children.*
- *Never henna your hair if you use any of the other colouring agents, or if you have grey hair. The henna will enter the cortex, change the pigments dramatically, resulting in that ugly orange-red colour, especially around the front and sides, which is often difficult to correct.*
- *Read and follow the instructions on the label carefully.*
- *Always condition your hair before colouring, especially the ends. This seals the cuticles and prevents the cortex from absorbing too much colour. Condition after colouring, as well.*
- *Don't subject your hair to the double chemical action of colouring and relaxing simultaneously. Wait at least six weeks between processes, and preferably use temporary or semi-permanent colouring.*
- *Remember that the sun can affect your hair colour, if you relax or dye your hair. Wear a hat or head-tie.*

TEMPORARY COLOURS

Colour rinses, sprays and crayons are the easiest to apply and remove, and also the safest, as they colour only the cuticle without entering and damaging the cortex. They are fantastic for a quick lift, for a big night out, or a change of your persona. Here is the opportunity to try out all those psychedelic colours either over your whole head or in streaks. A splash of gold or bronze can look stunning with an evening dress or traditional cloth.

Temporary colouring washes out after each shampoo, and can rub off on clothing or pillow cases. So if you are trying out those coloured sparkles, watch out that yours is a blameless life! As long as you have a good supply, these are the safest to colour your hair, as they are acidic, and therefore work well with the natural acidity of the hair. They mask grey hair effectively, and bring out or contrast dramatically with your natural hair colour.

SEMI-PERMANENT COLOURS

These go a step further by penetrating the cuticle, the hairs' natural coating, without entering the cortex and changing the colour pigments. So they will not drastically change hair colour, but they will mask grey hair. The colour usually lasts up to five shampoos, and is a safe process, to be recommended.

PERMANENT COLOURING OR STREAKING

Such processes enter the cuticle and change the structure of the hair, altering its colour through a wide range, though it is advisable to stick to the colours devised for black hair, rather than turn your raven locks blonde! The colour lasts until the hair grows out, and they cover grey hair effectively. But the roots re-growth has to be touched-up monthly, unless you have it streaked; and your hair will need a lot of deep conditioning. Permanent colouring is nowadays easy to apply at home due to the simplicity of the instructions.

GOING STRAIGHT

THE HOT COMB

Although the natural comb originated in Africa, our ingenious Black American sister, Madam C.J. Walker, invented the iron comb. This has increased the styling possibilities of our hair, by giving us creative options, allowing us to change quickly in and out of our normal curliness. No wonder she died as the first Black millionairess.

The hot comb is still very popular, though we now have the electric pressing comb. Any hot comb can fry your hair or burn your scalp. Watch out also for scalp burns caused by an excess of hot oil dripping onto it.

IMPORTANT PRECAUTIONS

- *Never press your hair yourself without first being shown the proper way to do it. Your hairdresser or an experienced friend may be helpful.*

Three hairstyles created with straightened hair.

The instructions for creating this style are given on p. 154.

- *Press only clean and conditioned hair, but never when it is wet.*
- *Use pressing oil or pressing cream, not oils to lubricate or condition your hair, as they don't have enough wax in them, for effective pressing. Don't apply too much of the pressing oil or cream to your scalp; put it on lightly onto your hair, paying attention to the delicate ends of your hair. Lightly oil your scalp, when you have completed the pressing.*
- *Always test the comb on a folded pad of newspapers before touching your hair with it. If the paper turns brown, the comb is too hot.*
- *Your operation area should be well-lit with a large mirror, or preferably two, to enable you to see the back of your head.*
- *After pressing, give your scalp a quick massage while still warm, using a little oil or cream. Comb or brush gently, styling with rollers or wearing it straight.*
- *The frequency of hot combing depends on how often you wash your hair. But consider giving your hair a rest now and again, by alternating with the natural look.*

CHEMICAL RELAXERS

Relaxing the hair has swept through Black societies, just like bleaching creams did. While bleaching is dying a slow but sure death, because of the danger posed to our health and the acceptance that Black Is Beautiful, relaxers are gaining in popularity, as they give Black women endless opportunities to transform their naturally curly hair into different styles. They offer such creative freedom, that they have transcended the 'conked' look of the Black Americans of a generation ago, who felt economically and socially impelled to look like whites. Relaxed hair is easily managed, can be styled in a great variety of ways; you can swim, sweat profusely or get caught in the rain, without your straightened style reverting to its natural curliness.

But like all processed hair, relaxed hair must be devotedly cared for. Before you start, make sure that you will be able to give it the necessary care, because there's no turning back. A change back to natural will have to wait until after the life of the head of hair that has been relaxed.

The relaxer works by loosening the cuticle, causing it to swell, so that the chemical can penetrate into the inner cortex layer, where it actually rearranges the keratin chains in a new straighter relationship to each other. This makes the hair straight or less curly. Relaxer usually contains less than 2.5% of sodium hydroxcide (lye), which acts fast and effectively.

	Product strength	Relaxing time
Fine hair	Mild	8 minutes
Medium hair	Regular	10 minutes
Very thick hair	Super	15 minutes

But each relaxer differs and contains more or less lye, so never leave it on beyond the times stipulated, or the hair and scalp will be damaged. After the set time, a neutraliser is applied to stop the process and fix the hair in its new straight molecular structure. The hair must be conditioned after every shampoo and there are special conditioners available for relaxed hair; otherwise you can use any of the rich protein conditioners.

If the relaxer has permanently straightened the hair that has emerged to the surface of the scalp, what about natural curly new growths? These too must be relaxed by a re-touch of the roots, after about three months; otherwise the hair will break at the junction of the straight and curly, a common cause of hair loss – and you can't blame the product. Hair-relaxing is best done by a fully-trained and qualified hairdresser, in a reputable salon.

You should let your hairdresser know what other processing your hair has been subjected to, as on no account should chemical relaxer be used on recently dyed hair. Keep the ends well-trimmed and don't have your hair relaxed more than three or four times a year. Don't touch up new growths with a hot comb, and remember to cover your relaxed hair when in the sun, due to its damaging effect on all processed hair.

A great diversity of styles.

STYLING

Nowhere in the world is the language of hair-styles and hair decoration more expressive, fabulous and diverse than in Africa, where women's hair has become the focus of adornment, the height of artistic expression and a powerful tool of sexual attraction. It is therefore not surprising that in 1978, Nigeria's Franca Afegbua won the coveted trophy at the International Hairdressers' Convention in London, for a fantastic performance, originality and creativity.

Hairdressing is a big social event in an African woman's calendar; it can take the whole day, and usually implies a visit to a friend or relative, to help out. During this time, she will be catching up on all the news, eating a special meal, and playing with the children.

Back-stage with Franca Afegbua and her award-winning team for Salon '78 in London.

A thread-wrapped creation by Franca Afegbua.

Franca Afegbua, Nigerian hairdresser, with the cup she won 'for a fantastic performance by the first African artistic hair-styling team.'

A close-cut Afro.

Another Afro cut.

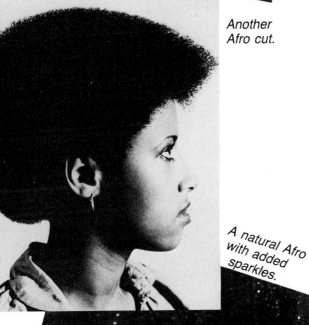

A natural Afro with added sparkles.

Contemporary African hairstyles range from the bald mud-covered look of the Masai woman, through shaved hair patterns, to elaborate braiding and the Western style of relaxed hair. Traditional African hairstyles have influenced the world hair fashion scene and will continue to do so. Witness the way white women plait their hair like ours and the use of mud plasters in various colours. As fashions and cultures interchange we all have the right to wear our hair in the style of our choice. Hair-straightening is *not* a black wish to look white; to be able to extend the range of our creativity and enjoyment of fashion is part of the pleasure of being a woman.

STYLE OPTIONS

Your clothes and hair characterise your style. Fashion in both is always changing, so keep an eye on the trends; experiment and discover the styles that suit you. Be guided by your lifestyle, age, height, size and facial shape – and of course – your hair type. The style you choose should be comfortable and manageable, so that you don't have to rush back constantly to the hairdresser for re-styling.

Let's begin with the bald look. A Black American relative of mine, living in New York, once shaved off all her hair. With her broad brow, high cheekbones and forehead, she looked stunning. The only trouble was that people kept lovingly stroking her head; 'For good luck' they claimed. Her hairstyle is now a sculpted Afro! The bald look may solve all your hair problems, but you need a perfectly-shaped skull and body to balance, and wonderful facial structure. Remember to protect your head from extremes of temperature.

THE SCULPTED AFRO

This style needs regular trimming, especially at the ends, and also proper combing. For easy combing, moisten your hair with equal parts of water and oil, or a spray. You can untangle it with your fingers, before combing. A big Afro looks top-heavy on a tiny woman, and also looks a bit old-fashioned.

WEAVE-ON

A process that should only be undertaken by professionals. 'Weave on' has become a common phenomenon among Black women, especially for making thin hair thick, or short hair long, or as a remedy for partial baldness, or for those wanting a completely new look. It is a process in which strands of hair are actually finely sewn onto the roots of clean hair in thin layers, using a special needle and thread. The hair is then cut and styled.

Because hair grows at least an inch every month, a re-tightening must be done after three months, when the process is repeated, this time at the root of the new growth. It is expensive, because real hair is best. If the correct colour, texture and technique are used, the result should be secure, not look artificial and there should be no hair damage.

During the weave on process.

After weave on.

Plaiting on stage during Franca Afegbua's award-winning performance at Wembley.

PLAITING OR WEAVING

This style is often wrongly referred to as 'weave on'. It is the most common African style, dating from antiquity, which has been modified in different areas, to suit regional culture. A variation is the corn row. Never have your plaits done too tight, it can pull your hair out. Because they last a long time, the style is ideal for those who don't want to worry about re-styling. However, it must be well maintained.

Shampoo in much the same way as usual, being careful not to rub too vigorously, so as not to undo the plaits. Because you don't comb or brush your hair every day, the scalp should be gently massaged. Don't wear this style for more than two months at the most, and remember to shampoo any added hair pieces. A natural hair piece is best as it enables you to curl and style the plaits in many Western styles as well as traditional.

One of the plaited styles created by Franca Afegbua, with added cowrie shells and beads.

A Nigerian woman plaits her friend's hair.

THREAD WRAPPING

An equally popular African style, in which black cotton thread, specially produced for the purpose, is wound tightly round strands of hair. The hair is then parted in different styles to make elaborate constructions. Remember that it is one of the commonest causes of traction alopaecia or hair loss.

A young girl from Eastern Nigeria with a thread-wrapped style.

Another thread wrapped style.

Lurex thread and added beads create stage glamour for this Black British singer.

STYLING AIDS

In Africa, various types of hair attachments, wigs, moulds and frames have been used to enhance hair styling down the centuries. Ancient Egyptians used elaborate wigs, which denoted rank. At first they were of real hair, but in later history, there were additions of palm, raffia, fibre and wool, along with a wide selection of colours, which bore no semblance to reality. To this day the Fulani girls of northern Nigeria are given false pieces of hair, passed down from generation to generation, which are woven into their own, and bound with gold and other ornaments.

Some traditional African styles require the use of a foundation of cloth, fibre padding or arched bamboo supports, to form a high cap-shaped hair style. Then the hair is oiled, rubbed with camwood paste or clay mixed with indigo, and arranged over the mould. It is then smeared with palm oil, to give a greenish tinge and make it sparkle in the sunlight. This is a traditional style for brides in some areas, for priestesses in others. Such an elaborate style must be protected from the rain and when lying down, so a carved wooden cushion placed under the neck, helps to retain the coiffure. 'Yanga get pain' means 'Being fashionable is painful.' As far as hair is concerned it need not be so nowadays, though many plaited styles are time-consuming to say the least. Four hours is the very minimum you can expect to devote to such works of art.

WIGS

Wigs can make you as fashionable as you want, without suffering, except possibly from the heat. Simply choose the right texture, style, fit and colour to suit the various aspects of your life style. But as you get older, buy wigs with a touch of grey to match your maturing face. They are made from either expensive human hair, or man-made (synthetic) fibres. Black women don't usually like to part with their precious hair, so the human hair is usually obtained from Orientals or Caucasians, somewhat different from our own hair texture, therefore with the risk of looking artificial unless superbly treated.

Synthetic wigs are cheaper, long-lasting and can be shampooed without losing their curl, because the style has been baked in. In fact nowadays, good 'artificial' wigs can look as natural as real hair ones.

Your wig should fit well, but not tightly, and blend with your hair line. A stretch or open cap base are best, especially in hot climates. You are also able to scratch your head. Try camouflaging the hairline of you wig by wearing it not like a cap, but behind your natural hair line, then combing and blending your own hair into the wig. Today, there are good wigs made by Black manufacturers that have a natural hair line for the front and sides of the head.

Before putting the wig on, have your hair neatly plaited, or wrapped with thread, or in a corn row style, though of course, it must not bulge under the wig. Put the wig on from the front to the back, securing with hairpins, one on either side, at the front, back and top of your head. Try not to wear a scarf or head tie tightly over your wig, as it spoils the shape.

Wigs should not be worn all the time, at least not in hot climates or weather; no matter how airy the base of the wig is. It's rather like wearing a bathing cap all the time, and can cause sweating to the extent of scalp irritation. So let your hair and scalp enjoy some fresh air now and then. Never share wigs, it is dangerously unhygenic. Your own hair should be kept scrupulously clean and conditioned, and not just because you don't want to be disgraced, should your wig ever come off accidentally!

Wig care

Take care of your wig as you would your own hair, especially wigs made of natural hair, which are very delicate. The cleaning, shampooing and styling should be done by a professional hairdresser.

Synthetic wigs are easier to care for, and good ones come with clear instructions, which should be followed if you want your wig to look fresh and attractive.

CHAPTER 8

AFRICAN FASHION GOES INTERNATIONAL

A fabulous Ghanaian Up and Down in hand-woven silk Kente cloth.

In some traditional African societies, clothes are believed to be magic in origin, and intended to protect the sex parts from the eyes of evil spirits, ill-wishers or the envious. A woman had to be particularly careful and ensure that evil spirits did not enter her body. So the need arose for a first elementary garment, which was probably made from vegetable fibres, and used as a sort of primitive sanitary belt.

Clothing also expressed the basic human desire for adornment, particularly in areas where there was no strong tradition in body decoration. Within each African country, within each tribe, and often from one area to another inhabited by those people, African fashion is highly individualistic. Each sub-division has its own way of dressing, its own cloths, its own craft techniques – of beading, embroidery, leatherwork and so on, and its own jewellery. Nomadic peoples tend to pay even more attention to splendid personal adornment than those long settled in an urban environment, fulfilling the inbuilt creativity of the human species on themselves, rather than on elaborate palaces, temples and homes. People on the move with their flocks, such as the Berbers of North Africa, have highly-developed skills in silver jewellery, or the Turkanas of East Africa in beading their garments of beaten bark cloth.

The Ahouach dancers of Berber origin now living in Morocco with their spangled clothes.

A Moroccan silk Kaftan.

Bark is beaten then embroidered with beads to form clothing by the Turkanas of East Africa.

AFRICAN FASHION TODAY

For simplicity's sake, let's take a look at the evolution and influence of four traditional types of dress which best characterise the way women dress nowadays, following the cultural precepts of their ancestors. These are:

- *The Wrapper.*
- *The Up and Down.*
- *The Kaftan.*
- *The Boubou.*

HOW THE WRAPPER EVOLVED

In East Africa, the wrapper tends to be worn over the breasts, leaving the shoulders bare, in the West, it is worn around the waist, accompanied by a blouse, and often much flirtatious wrapping and re-wrapping, while dancing, or even walking along. In most places, the wrapper evolved through history in the following manner:

- *The first female covering of vegetable fibre, like pants.*
- *The short skirt. A flat or pleated piece of cloth, sewn onto a band and worn by young girls until after puberty and marriage. Young female children often wear only attractive waist beads, which are then exposed over the band as they grow older.*
- *The skirt, cloth or wrapper. At puberty, about five metres of cloth are wrapped over the short skirt, or petticoat, draped to the left side to cover the calves or ankles. In some rural societies, the breasts remain uncovered. The size and number of the waist beads is increased, worn under the skirt, adding a touch of sensuality in many cultures.*
- *The second skirt, cloth or wrapper. In some areas a second wrapper is tied over the first one, again draped to the left, but tied to cover the breasts, exposing the first wrapper underneath. This is worn by married women and used to support babies on their backs, and often made of an alternative, more porous material, when used for this function. Otherwise, the royal wives in some of the courts of traditional West African kings, such as the Oba of Benin, wear the two wrappers in white, offset by masses of coral jewellery.*
- *The stole. A small cloth in the same material, folded and laid usually over the left shoulder.*
- *The blouse. Two rectangles joined as sleeves and sewn to the edges of a larger third one, which has been folded to fit the bodice loosely, with a huge oval neckline, cut from the fold, leaving the shoulders wide, unpadded and seamless. Fashions in blouses change. When the*

Wrapper and stole.

A wrapper and stole in woven fabric as worn by the Yorubas of Nigeria

wrapper is of printed material, the blouse is usually of the same fabric. But when it is of woven cloth, the fashion was colourful broderie anglaise blouses, or figured embroidered lace, often of silk crepe. But with the ban on the importation of this lace (to save foreign exchange), the fashion emphasis is now on an embroidered blouse of the same woven fabric as the wrapper – or the newest fashion – a wrapper and embroidered blouse of Adire, the locally-dyed indigo cloth.

● The headtie. The method of tying expresses artistic flair, mood and age, and the angle at which it is tilted on the head, reveals a young woman's intentions. Pushed to the front and tilted to one side, means: 'I am ready for anything,' in some parts of Africa!

The traditional fabric for this outfit today is usually expensive, hand-woven cloth of heavy cotton, sometimes sparkled with lurex thread, called Asooke in Nigeria. Worn with a dazzling display of gold jewellery and coral or other semi-precious beads, this is high fashion for special occasions among the Yoruba. For traditional ceremonies and festivals, a whole compound of families or an extended family, will be dressed in matching fabric, the women in their total outfits, the men in long flowing robes, trousers and hat, all alike. A great deal of money is expended in this way. Young married girls assume an air of responsibility, confidence and maturity, when they emerge in this formal outfit.

The mode of tying and draping the wrapper varies from one African country to another, and even from tribe to tribe. Many of our Black American and West Indian sisters have asked for step by step instructions on how to tie the headtie and wrapper, so here's how the Yoruba do it:-

THE HEADTIE

For a dramatic effect and easy styling, stiff material like taffeta is best, though there are fabrics specially made in Africa for headties. You require a piece about two metres long and 1 metre wide. Pleat lengthways, equally into three sections. Standing in front of your mirror, place the centre of the headtie against the back of your head, and bring both ends to the front. Cross over firmly and tie in a knot at the back.

Style by gently pulling out different parts of the headtie, to suit your fabric, mood and occasion, using pins to hold your creation in place. For the final touch, simply tilt the headtie gently to one side, and slightly forwards.

An alternative method is to begin from the front of the head, crossing over at the back and then tying the ends at the side. Once the headtie is secure, you can move it around on your head until you find the shape, style and angle that suits you.

A richly coloured headtie from Nigeria.

The 'I am ready for anything' headtie in heavily embroidered Adire.

Nigerian headtie in colourful stiff fabric called hayes

Creative tying of a cotton print from Ghana.

Another method of tying a large
cotton headtie in African print.

An Adire cloth twisted around
matches an Indigo tie-dyed T shirt.

The small headtie.

Tying the headtie and wrapper, step-by-step.

Always play around with the knotted end. The position of this can add panache.

The small headtie

Usually worn with an Up and Down or a Boubou. You need a piece of cloth about one and a half metres long and 45 cm wide (usually of the same fabric as the outfit.) Twist lengthways and simply tie round the head in a butterfly knot at the back. Ease towards the brow. Two colours of plain cloth twisted together make an interesting contrast to the outfit.

TYING THE WRAPPER

You need two and a half metres of cloth, about one and a quarter metres wide, and preferably in the same fabric as the Buba (blouse.) Fold the cloth according to the length you want. Stand with feet apart and begin wrapping from the back, holding the wrapper over the Buba.

Tuck the end in your left hand into the right side of your waist. Bring the end in your right hand over the left side, and tuck securely into the waist. An optional safety procedure is to tie a narrow piece of cloth around your waist, concealing it in the folds. This holds the wrapper firmly in position.

An Up and Down in Lagos print with ruffled taffeta sleeves by the late Nigerian designer Joyce Obong.

THE UP AND DOWN

This is one of the most popular styles among West African women, especially urban ones, and lends itself most easily to the switchbacks of fashion change. These include the halterneck, strapless, sleeveless or backless, or featuring exaggerated sleeves. The top is worn over an ankle-length skirt. The style of this skirt varies from a wrapper tied to hug the hips, or a more or less tight-fitting sewn skirt with side slits, or an inset pleat to allow for easy leg movement.

Usually a tailor is employed to produce a bespoke garment, closely following the curves of its owner. The Up and Down is seen every day on the streets, and at offices and parties, but not at important traditional events.

Joyce Obong used a combination of print from Kaduna with woven Aso oke detail.

North African Kaftan.

THE KAFTAN

The kaftan is a long, loose, flowing robe, usually with a round or boat-shaped neck, and long or elbowlength loose sleeves. Originally, the kaftan swept down into Africa, with the Muslim Jihad, and nowadays it is popular with big women, in pregnancy, and for hostessing informal parties, or just to relax around the house. Black Americans took it over the waters, as part of the symbolism of Black Power. Like the Up and Down, it is usually made up in cool lightweight fabrics, many of which are creatively tie-dyed or made of batik in flowing silk or cotton. Of course there are wonderful African prints as well, and the fabric which has had such a great revival recently – Adire. Many kaftans are rich in embroidery around the neck and sleeves.

THE BOUBOU

The Boubou is found more in Francophone West African countries, such as Senegal and the Ivory Coast, where they specialise in sensational tie-dyed satin. To see a woman walking along in a Boubou is a matter of poetry, as the voluminous swirls sail out, particularly if it is made of a delicate fabric like silk, lace or voile.

Believe it or not, the origin of this style has been traced to the clothes worn by herdsmen in the deserts, to protect themselves against extremes of temperature, sand storms and winds. Today's sophisticated effect is very much dependant on the way you carry yourself in it, for instance nonchalantly holding one corner of the long overdress up to display a skirt of the same fabric beneath. Being essentially an overdress, unlike the kaftan, it has more variations on the theme – the overdress can be tucked into the band of the skirt of matching or toning material. The Boubou also differs from the kaftan in that it is usually made of expensive fabrics so it is dressier, and also cut fuller.

A Sarong-style skirt in African print.

INFLUENCES ON AFRICAN FASHION

Various factors have played a significant role in the evolution of clothing on the African continent. Among them have been political and climatic conditions, which have modified or characterised the various forms of nudity. In some hot parts of tropical and sub-tropical Africa almost complete nudity was and still is practised, though for the majority of these peoples, the genitals are covered. Interestingly, such minimal forms of dress are often compensated by elaborate decorative attention to the rest of the body, which often involve permanent structural alteration. The women living on the Benue plateau of Nigeria wear large gold lip-plugs; the Masai of Kenya stretch their ear-lobes to amazing lengths, inserting huge earrings.

Other influences on the evolution of clothing on the African continent were mainly religious and through trading. Christianity and Islam both demanded body covering, to conform with their concepts of modesty and the removal of temptation. So they provided models from other cultures for covering the body, and in some countries, like Zimbabwe, succeeded so completely in shaming the locals out of their original clothing, that the indigenous craft of bark-cloth preparation, has almost died out. Very little remains of pre-Christian clothing on the backs of modern Zimbabweans. Under Christian influence, European and American missionaries were busy converting the people, not only to Christianity, but also to Western culture, its clothing, styles and fabrics. Those converted to Islam adopted the various kinds of trousers associated with an equestrian society, with short or long flowing tops for the men and complete coverage for the women.

The effect of trading with the Portuguese, Dutch and British also significantly affected the clothes along the coastal areas. However, various local innovations developed and modified the clothes worn today, and one's faith does not necessarily influence one's mode of dress any more. The famous and figure-flattering Up and Down was developed in Ghana as a fine compromise

A Western-style shirt-dress designed in his own fabric by Olujimi.

between the demands of Christian modesty and a subtle way of displaying a nicely turned posterior. Many practising Muslims in sub-Saharan Africa dress as their non-Muslim sisters do, and have not taken up the complete covering of either historical or modern Fundamentalism.

Clothing is an unspoken language, charged with subtle, impressive power and messages that words do not possess. The image you create by your clothing influences how others perceive you, and delivers a unique message about you. This particular use of clothing is very significant in traditional African societies, elements of which persist today, in spite of outside influences. Messages are conveyed by clothing about such things as the birth of a baby and its sex, the woman's status, the completion of various initiation ceremonies, her availability for marriage, bereavement, menopause and so on. Variations in African clothing have always given many more signals than in Western society; the great exception being the black mourning clothes worn in Europe and America.

As an effective means of communication, clothing in the traditional context also gives immediate information about nationality, culture and religion, with far greater regional variety than in many other parts of the world. This could be due as much to an innate African love of and flair for personal creativity in appearance as to the desire to communicate!

To this day, clothing serves as a means of self-expression, a reflection of our personalities, and how we feel about ourselves. Whether you wear traditional or Western clothing, or mix the two; dress for yourself, please yourself, play up your body's best attributes. Don't count on making an impression on men or on other women. They may not even notice, or they may misconstrue your intentions!

WHAT IS FASHION?

I cannot find a more suitable definition than the one used by Coco Chanel, that remarkable female designer, whose influence is still strong in international fashion. She says: 'Fashion is that thing which is soon out of fashion!' That swooping hem-line, the baggy long trousers, that we named 'Keep Lagos clean' in Nigeria, the headtie that aimed for the sky, all pass like the seasons. Fashion is a reflection of its time, and contemporary society in each country always offers a wide range and choice of clothes to suit different lifestyles. Apart from national costume, the style which is preserved as part of a country's cultural heritage, which itself undergoes differences in interpretation, what is fashionable today may look dated tomorrow.

In talking about fashion for Black women, we shall consider both international and African fashion, because we should be aware of what's happening on the world fashion scene, as well as in our own countries, to enable us to create our own individual style.

Haute couture or high fashion is created by its designers and those who wear the clothes. The women could be film stars, models or simply those that can afford couturier clothes. The success or failure of a style depends on how the models impress the fashion buyers, who come to the bi-annual Collections, to assess how the style will then translate down-market, in cheaper versions for the high street shops. Fashion magazines and the media help to promote the current tenets

An Ahouach woman of North Africa lifting part of her lace dress to form a veil.

of design and beauty. But the autocratic power of the great couturiers of Paris, Rome, London and latterly New York, has waned.

Nowadays 'street fashion', the creative self-expression of people who may be unemployed (rather than swanning around on yachts in designer swimwear), is a force to be reckoned with. The elements of 'street fashion' have been culled from a multitude of sources, including Punk music and other semi-political forms of protest. These dynamic social forces have created a whole new alternative style of dress. Street fashion is created by people whose life styles are quite other than the world of high couturier fashion – and the famous designers have had to listen. The Japanese created The Bag Lady Look to reflect a more casual way of life, where loose-fitting clothes and comfort are the order of the day.

AN HISTORICAL PERSPECTIVE

Before the introduction of machine technology, when cloth was woven and sewn by hand, fashion changed slowly. Royalty and the aristocracy showed their power and wealth by wearing clothing of expensive cloth, which was elaborately embroidered and embellished with jewels. In those troubled times, it was not always safe to expose precious belongings in public, because of the risk of robbery, and so the cloak evolved in the West.

In societies where women were (and in some cases they still are) treated as possessions, a man might well consider his wife or wives to be his most prized ones. To minimise the danger of losing a wife, convention dictates that when she ventures out, she covers her face with a veil and her body with austere clothing. Extreme modesty is believed to avoid exciting lust in men. Beneath the unremarkable cover, these women often wear attractive clothes and make-up, which in some cases are visible, and are probably all the more provocative as they are glimpsed rather than seen openly.

By the beginning of this century, Paris had become the centre of international fashion, where new designs were created for a handful of wealthy society women. Europe had a negligible Black population and the 12% of the US population did not have the money to participate in 'best-dressed' lists. Fashion conscious black or poorer white women took cuttings from magazines to their local dressmakers to copy, a practice which is still followed in Africa. Fashion filtered through very slowly to the poor of Europe and America, so they tended to keep to their traditional clothes. By the 1930's the film industry was persuading the great designers to create clothes for their productions, and gradually the influence of Hollywood became apparent in the shops for a growing number of cinema-goers.

During the Second World War, the centre of fashion moved

to the USA, and by the time liberated Paris had regained its traditional role as a fashion leader, there had been a social and economic revolution. Fashion had become big business. Its leaders were willing to promote ready-to-wear and later – even mass-produced clothes where the signature of the designer could be equated with the price tag. Designer fashion was born. Obviously the more frequently clothes and cosmetic fashions changed, the better it was for business.

But at the same time the consciousness was growing that Black beauty was not recognized, let alone appreciated. African countries considered such competitions as Miss World degrading to women or immodest. A valid fear was that African entrants would be judged by Western standards, and would therefore be at a disadvantage.

The creators of fashion were mostly men, and until the 1920s and again in the 1950s, Chanel introduced some sanity into fashion. She freed women by creating clothes in which they could live, breathe, feel comfortable – and youthful.

SWINGING LONDON

A decade later, Mary Quant, the British designer, dressed *young* women in defiance of the opinion of other top designers, that: 'A woman does not learn to dress well until she is over 35.' Coming at a time when London was swinging, and Brown Sugar was sweet to more than just the Rolling Stones – when Black women were at last acknowledged to have their own kind of beauty, younger women, both black and white, could at last afford fashion that was truly created for their life styles. It was a clothing revolution, underpinned by various photographers, their famous models and film-makers, in which no longer did young women struggle to look older – that is, to fit in with a media image of a 'sophisticated' woman, with a white powdered face, dark red lipstick, and poured into the obligatory 'little black dress'. Fashion was never to be the same again, because at last women could do their thing, choose their style, and not feel inadequate if they could not afford, copy or live up to the dictates of the couturiers.

BLACK FASHION CONSCIOUSNESS

By now Blacks in the USA were well-advanced in their struggle for civil rights and had considerable spending power. Europe, and especially England, had a recognized Black minority group and African states, having attained independence, had sophisticated diplomats and wealthy citizens, who were as much at home in Paris, London or New York, as in their own countries. The time was ripe for fashion, cosmetics and hair products which suited Black women.

A shirt-dress in his own transfer
fabric by the Nigerian designer
Olujimi.

A vast range of make-up had been created for white women, and that was that. Black women had to contend with unsuitable shades of foundation, eye shadow and lipsticks and struggled to look white or 'acceptable', by wearing Caucasian-style wigs or straightening their hair.

In 1964, a six foot Black model, Donyale Luna, snarling, crouching with hands crooked like claws, as though she were about to spring (a symbol of aggression associated with the Black Power movement – the Black Panthers) exploded onto the pages of fashion magazines. She became the first Black female model, an international star, and opened the door for other Black models to enter the world fashion arena. It was a completely new image for Black women, the 'Fashion Negress'. Although all this implied a degree of success for Black women, many of them were unhappy about the way their photographs were used merely for impact as exotic, freakish creatures on which to display the designer's most outrageous fashion. It was not a desirable role-model for the majority of Black women.

A Sierra Leonese cotton print becomes an urbanised version of classical African style.

Although glamorous, sexy, Black entertainers, like Josephine Baker, Lena Horne and the Supremes, were also achieving prominence, many Black women were still 'conking' their hair and bleaching their skin in an attempt to look white.

Earlier in the decade, the South African singer, Miriam Makeba, had toured the USA, wearing her hair cropped short in the style of her homeland. Then an attractive Black American actress, Cecily Tyson, appeared on US television with the same short, natural haircut, taking great pride in her pure negroid look. The Afro style had arrived. It was exciting and significant because for the first time, Black women in the USA had a style of their own, which became a symbol of the new pride in their race. The Afro look and James Brown were announcing: 'I'm Black and proud.'

'BLACK IS BEAUTIFUL'

By 1968, the phrase 'Black is Beautiful' was coined. From then on, Black women were featured more and more in the public eye, not just as entertainers, or models; sensual, exotic and glamorous objects of the white man's sexual fantasies, but as intelligent thinkers and achievers. These women became politicians, leaders in the professions and also – civil rights activists. In 1968 Shirley Chisholm became the first Black woman to be elected to the US Congress, and Corretta King, determined, defiant and hardworking, carried on the struggle for which her husband had died. But it was the young challenging Angela Davis, in her big Afro hairstyle, who most clearly showed the world the new image of the Black woman.

Suddenly it was fashionable to be Black and everyone wanted to be a 'Soul Sister'. Cecily Tyson introduced the traditional African corn-row plaiting to the American public. It was a tremendous success and yet again boosted the message that 'Black is Beautiful'. Young whites of both sexes came to adopt the Afro hairstyle, using perms and wigs as necessary. Then in the 1970's the Paris designers introduced a variety of African ethnic concepts, ranging from fabrics like batik, kangas and kitengs to turbanned heads and heavy jewellery.

At about the same time, as more African countries became independant, Africans themselves renewed their interest and pride in their traditional fashion, textiles and decorative arts. Many Black Americans were reaching towards Africa for cultural identity, adopting various forms of African dress. Black American women began wearing headties, kaftans and braided hair, as cultural fashion.

Of course there are many more battles for Black women to win, but thanks to the struggles of those pioneers, we have at least been accepted as who we are. The proponents of 'Black

is Beautiful' fought for Black identity and won. Black female models are today top of the international lists, and no longer have to look like freaks or whites. One particular model who pioneered this new image is Naomi Sims, who has always been committed to her colour. She usually wears her hair in a refined Afro and her make-up has the right dark shades that enhance her natural good looks. She says: 'Black women have captured the limelight and we are here to stay. Being a Black female should be considered an asset.'

FASHION TRENDS

Nowadays Black women can choose to wear whatever style they like, from whatever source. That attraction to the exotic in dress fabrics and jewellery among high fashion designers in the '70s, coincided with the tendency for fashion to move upwards from the streets, rather than downwards from the haute couture salons. Rigid dress codes have relaxed and, reflecting evolving life styles, emphasise individuality of expression and style. At last 'anything goes.' New fashion ideas spring up daily and every woman has become her own designer, putting together her unique appearance. For the young in particular, street fashion has found a ready stage and audience, for dressing controversially is an essential part of the generation game. Today street fashion has more influence on what real women wear, than anything else, London being the centre.

Fashion is a game of imagination and creativity. Unconsciously, or in a rejection of the fashion and values of the previous generation, it was the young who came out with alternative style, sometimes off-beat innovations not always accepted by the commercial market. Real Punk, with its strong tribal motifs, Mohican fluorescent coloured hair, body decorations (or mutilations) and jungle patterns are still sufficiently unusual and startling as to turn heads, even on London's Kings Road. Punk fashion is not common among Black women, though of course body decorations and 'jungle' patterns are not new to us. However, the brilliant colour sprays we use on our hair for parties (owing its debt to Punk), and a large slice of street fashion *have* been adopted by young Black women.

Fashion in Africa has never been a matter of the top designers dictating what we wear, as was the case in the West. As we have seen, each individual African country has its own unique mode of 'traditional' and 'modern traditional' wear, the latter being the sophisticated urbanised version of the former. Fashion trends are introduced more by individual pace-setters, dressmakers, sewing mistresses and tailors, who are geniuses with a pair of scissors, turning out the most fantastic designs without patterns or sketches.

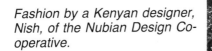

Fashion by a Kenyan designer,
Nish, of the Nubian Design Co-
operative.

Trousers and shirt in his own
fabric by Olujimi.

A jump-suit in woven Aso oke
fabric by Nigerian Onyeka
Onwenu.

Traditional fabrics from various Nigerian states.

Joyce Obong called this outfit 'Nsa' or Mermaid.

The tailors pride themselves in their ability to reproduce Western-style suits, skirts, coats and so on. Many, like the sewing mistresses, also design and sew modern and traditional women's fashions. However, the sewing mistresses, not the tailors, have the upper hand in guiding, though never dictating the fashion trends.

AFRICAN INFLUENCE ON WORLD FASHION

There is now and again a noticeable African influence on international fashion. Africa casts a spell on summers, so designs are created usually in imitations of African prints, or subtly altered copies of our jewellery. Rarely, if ever, is the genuine article to be spotted, with the exception of the Dutch Wax kaftans and danshikis which raged through the West in the '70s. As the name suggests, the fabric Dutch Wax is not even produced in Africa, but mass produced abroad and exported to the continent, where, with an inverted sense of snobbishness, a 'real' Dutch wax, that is an imported one, is more prized than the local prints.

But we have a rich fashion heritage and a stunning variety of both traditional craft techniques in fashion and a superb range of machine prints to inspire us. Our great cultural advantages, history and traditions should give us great confidence. We should see ourselves at the centre of the fashion world, just as Japanese designers have been doing. In fact African designers have started to search for ideas sparked off by ethnic dress, art and craft, translating them into modern fashion. Sometimes they use local fabrics to create innovative Western styles. At other times they incorporate touches of Western fabric with the indigenous, to create variations on traditional styles. But all of them promote African fabric in their fashion. Designers like the Nubian Design Co-operative of Kenya, or the late Joyce Obong, House of Isis, African Connections, Chic Afrique, Shade boutique and Onyeka Onwenu of Nigeria, are giving a new meaning to the cosmopolitan flavour of today's very African fashion.

HOW TO CREATE STYLE

Whatever fashion we wear, the joy of dressing is that it allows us to express our individuality and display whatever talent we have for co-ordination and design. If we are looking at Western fashion, there are in effect two ways of dressing nowadays, according to your life style, age, preference – and usually – your pocket. One is by the classical route, with a few, 'good', carefully chosen items that are treated as investments, and to which you gradually add, in a co-ordinated way. The other is

the way many younger women dress – more outrageously perhaps, more creatively – arguably, and certainly more haphazardly. But although people cross from one side to the other, neither camp can afford to waste their money. If what you wear is of good quality (or looks as if it is), and has a certain rhythm from top to bottom, then you have style. Lacking in style is to be overdressed and weighed down with ostentatious gold jewellery. Those who suffer from poor posture are sadly lacking in style too. Some are born with style, others can develop their own sharp, chic, self-confident image.

I learnt about fashion from my mother at a very early age. A sewing-mistress who comes from a royal African family, she always epitomises a certain elegance. Her clothes are simple, well co-ordinated and never astonishing. She taught my sisters and I that being elegant means that your bra straps are clean and well-concealed, your clothes, headtie or hat do not need constant adjusting, your shoes are not pinching, and that you move gracefully. You should be so comfortable in what you are wearing that you are unaware of it.

Style is difficult to define, because whatever the fashion you are wearing, it is an individual matter, which every woman hopes she has. Yet nobody can really pin it down to anyone else's satisfaction. Style is that personal touch that goes outside and beyond current fashion, which you give to your clothes, your personalised fashion with which you express your feelings, your personality and unique dress sense. It is natural, but not something that suddenly happens to you at eighteen. Your fashion environment and your own innate flair come slowly into play. You have fantasies as a child, and as you grow, they grow with you, until they mature and fit together.

Wealth has nothing to do with having style; you don't have to buy expensive clothes to be stylish. Nature sometimes creates a human being in such a way that no matter how well you dress her, she will still look like a masquerade, while there are women who can look very stylish in their oldest 'at home' dress. Style is therefore not just what we wear, how expensive or fashionable it is, but how we put our clothes, accessories, make-up and hairstyle together in harmony, our poise in using ingenious ideas and superb colours to enhance our skin colouring.

Style can't be bought, but it can be achieved. You can develop your own elegant personal style with a thorough going review of your choice of clothes in relation to your body structure; careful re-planning of your wardrobe and attention to accessories.

Traditional and Western fashion *can* be judiciously mixed and local jewellery *can* look fantastic with space-age clothes. My own favourite and repeated combination is to match the colour of my shoes and tights with the predominant colour of

An indigo kaftan with appliqué trim.

my traditional wrapper and blouse. The result is a slimming and lengthening effect to my small stature. When I dress in Western fashion, I still add a touch of African accessories, and keep to the same unbroken line of colour.

If like me, you feel you have found your style and feel happy and comfortable with it, congratulations. Stick with it, but from time to time, vary it, to move subtly with fashion trends. On the other hand, if you feel that you have not found your personal style, or that it could do with some improvement, let's set off on a voyage of discovery together.

THE JOURNEY TO ACHIEVING YOUR OWN STYLE

First always remember that fashion should reflect your mood, inspire you, but not dictate to you. Your sources of inspiration might be a model or an actress, an elegantly dressed woman at a chieftancy or wedding ceremony or – why not – that secretary on the bus who always looks so fresh. Don't be tempted to copy them, but use their ideas to create your own style. As your own fashion designer, you may well discover that you have some hidden talents yet unutilised, but you should have a rough idea of how you want to look, which includes:

- *Your cosmetics.*
- *Accessories like hats, headties, scarves, jewellery, shoes and handbags.*
- *Your dominant fashion image – traditional, modern African, Western, or a combination of fashions.*
- *Your hair style, whether woven, relaxed or natural etc.*

Conduct a style assessment on yourself, bearing in mind your height and figure, but don't feel limited by your age or profession. 'I am only a housewife' is the most damning self-introduction. Most African fashions can be worn by any age, unlike the mini-skirt, which is definitely for the young. Try experimenting with different looks, until you find a style that enhances your structure and compliments your personality. If you wish, ask the opinion of trusted friends, but remember that the decision is yours. Don't experiment with a new look before an important occasion or interview; you just won't feel confident and relaxed.

Mrs Ola Rotimi-Williams, an
excellent wife, mother and
hostess

MATURE STYLE

If you will not see forty again, it is perhaps time for your style
to speak softly, to be appropriate rather than astounding. In
dressing your age, you don't have to look dowdy or matronly.
In many African countries, a woman climbs the professional
and social ladder, gaining in importance and respect as she
matures. Fashion today offers a great variety of clothes for
women who are fit, and in good shape, not specifically for this
or that age, although the 'youth explosion' fashions are
inappropriate. Time to give your daughter those skin-tight jeans,
disco glitter and jewellery, mini skirts and fantasy make-up!

The best thing to do is to look for styles that will flatter your
maturing looks and still enable you to be elegant and graceful.
But don't make the mistake of sticking to the particular fashion
that suited you years ago; this is very dating. Move subtly with
the times and keep on enjoying yourself with fashion.

STYLE CAMOUFLAGE

Now is the time to bear your figure in mind, in clothes selection
for your style, playing up your good points and camouflaging the
bad ones. There are certain tricks you can play to give the
illusion of a better figure. Many African fashions hide a
multitude of sins, especially the loose kaftans or the wrapper
and blouse. But others, like the Western fashion of a narrow
skirt and fitted overblouse, do not look flattering on a woman
generously endowed at the hips. Here are a few guidelines for
common problems.

Neck

The neck is one of the early tell-tale areas of ageing. If you
need to do some camouflaging, or you have a long neck, high-
necked clothes are the obvious choice, or a scarf nonchalantly
tossed around the offending part. For a short neck, give
chokers a miss and wear instead long chains or beads or a
graded string of small beads. V-necklines are flattering.

Shoulders and arms

Shoulders are the part of your body that determine how all your
clothes hang on you and for designer-type clothes, this is a
significant aspect of style. For rounded forward curving
shoulders, raglan sleeves ie with no seam on the shoulder,
are flattering. Wide shouldered women should be happy, since
padded shoulders have been in fashion for some time. But
unless you don't mind looking like Superman, watch
exaggerated padding and fussy sleeves. Narrow shoulders
look wider in set-in sleeves or of course padded shoulders.

Fleshy arms do not look stylish if they are straining to burst out of tight sleeves; try soft draping. Three-quarter length or loose long sleeves with a wrist band are best. In hot weather, wear loose short sleeves, which should almost reach to your elbows. Most loose fitting African fashions that cover the shoulders are feminine in themselves and cover your feminine shape.

Breasts

Black women are reputed to be well endowed in this respect, but although this is arguably a racist fantasy, well shaped, well supported breasts certainly have sex appeal. If yours are on the generous side, wear a well-fitting bra with deep cups, but not so deep that you look matronly! Never wear anything clinging on your top half, rather loose-fitting or blouson tops, to balance your shape. Avoid square or polo necks, V-necklines are better for you, and you'll look absolutely regal in the Boubou. With small breasts, you have unlimited clothing options.

Waist

Flowing or wrapped African fashions in themselves tend to camouflage an expanding waistline, and only when we try to cram ourselves into a garment with a waist-band, do we realise the need to reform. But before the diet and exercise programme begins to pay its dividends, avoid gathered skirts, which look bulky, or busy prints and large patterns. Wear A-line or low-blousing dresses.

Hips

If you are generously endowed below the waist, give trousers a miss. Also, don't wear clinging fabrics or bright ones with large patterns. Dark plain colours give a slimming effect, and will flow and drape well in soft fabrics. Draw attention upwards with padded shoulders for balance and dominating jewellery. The wrapper and blouse or kaftan are disguises, but should not be excuses. Get into exercise!

Legs

Black women are reputed to have well proportioned legs and slim ankles. We are less pestered with varicose veins too. In fact when the designer Courrèges was launching his new short skirts in the 60s, he boldly announced that he was dedicating them to the negress: 'Because only the negro knee is perfectly proportioned.'

Ignoring fashion dictates, just drop or raise your hemline to suit the length and thickness of your legs, and of course, the

outfit. However, some designers, such as Saint Laurent, specifically recommend a length to balance the nature of his designs – for some years now – on the knee. (He also suggests wearing sheer black tights with just about everything but a bikini, and these are flattering to any leg size.) If you have short legs, avoid ankle straps. Sling-back shoes with a slight heel will give your legs a better line. Wear more trousers and clothes that cover your legs, in order to camouflage any leg defects.

Right or wrong

We all have an inner sense of what is right or wrong for us, when it comes to clothing. You try on something and you immediately feel awkward, outrageous or stunning in it. But you also have your favourite clothes that you wear again and again. There are combinations of figure problems, which will have to be solved individually, such as being short and fat, or short and thin, and so on. Just remember that wide women should avoid horizontal lines, which make them look fatter, while tall ones should not wear vertical lines, which are elongating.

DRESSING FOR THE OCCASION

Dressing for the occasion is sophisticated dressing. So many West African women dress up lavishly each day and for every occasion. The result is that we are either wrongly or overdressed. I have seen secretaries in Lagos offices dressed to kill in cocktail dresses! Create a wardrobe which is diverse enough to render service appropriate to the needs of the occasion and to suit your individual moods. If you are attending a traditional occasion, it may be out of place to wear Western fashion, like jeans or trousers, but for a family gathering, you don't have to arrive dripping in eighteen carat gold and the latest designer dress, or imported silk-crèpe wrapper.

Too often in Africa, sophisticated urban women visit relatives in villages, without toning down their appearance, to blend in with village life. This is bad manners and displays no sense of style. Your unique image may make heads turn in Dakar, Accra or New York, but it will cause jeers and embarrassment in a remote village, with a trail of inquisitive children behind you. So please remember that style should always remain appropriate.

ACCESSORIES

These are the items, those personal details, that sum up your style and uniqueness, putting the finishing touch to your image, and lifting your appearance out of the ordinary. They are used

Fez in Aso oke fabric by Pinky.

to harmonise with your individual features, your mood, clothing, hairstyle and skin colour. Naomi Sims says: 'Our colour is our best accessory.' We seem to have an innate understanding of the power of colours, which we should exploit.

Accessories include: scarves, shawls, stoles, headties, hats, handbags, belts, gloves, shoes, tights, hair decorations and of course the jewellery that we love so much. African fashion offers us a wide range of dramatic accessories. On the streets of London and Los Angeles, specialist shops are making a fortune from African accessories.

Accessories used properly can completely change the effect of an outfit, and their imaginative combination can enrich your basic wardrobe, giving you a different outfit each time. I sometimes wear rows of small, colourful African beads with a simple black dress, or local woven cloth in muted colours of browns and beige as a waistcoat, with an ivory coloured light-weight suit.

See your accessories as a good fashion investment, and buy them of excellent quality. This will add a look of luxury and taste to the simplest outfit. Classic accessories can last for years, adding style to the most flamboyant temporary fashion.

The question of balance is important. The accessories should be according to your size, shape and of course clothes. If you are small, scale down the size of your handbags, belts and jewellery. If you have a large frame, go for large shoulder bags, chunky jewellery, large scarves and belts. Keep the accessories to a minimum, with just one item commanding the total effect.

HATS

One very beautiful Nigerian hat that was formerly reserved for royalty and chiefs, is made of velvet, richly embroidered with metallic thread in the form of trails of leaves. Nowadays this type of hat looks fabulous on both sexes. Another option is the fez, an Islamic style, with a tassle of black silk. These hats, by virtue of the velvets and silks used, can look stunning with Western fashion. A plain cream-coloured suit in locally-woven fabric, with a bright silk blouse, topped by one of these colourful hats is an example of the way in which indigenous and imported fashion can be blended.

Some hats don't go well with a plaited hairstyle, and a beautifully constructed head-tie on top of long plaits looks frankly laughable. You can add trimmings for variation to simple straw, or natural flowers that remain fresh for some time, such as gardenias. Don't throw your old hats away; with a bit of imagination, you can create new styles from them. Try covering an old straw hat with suitable fabric to match a dressy outfit, or use the same material.

A Moroccan hat, worn with Nigerian bone jewellery.

Brooch by Betty Vaughan-Richards.

A Tissint woman from the Sahara region with her fabulous silver jewellery.

A Masai beaded necklace from East Africa.

Copper alloy pendants by Jinadu Oladepo on a batik cloth by Isaac Ojo, both from Oshogbo, Western Nigeria.

JEWELLERY

Women love jewellery, but I think Black women love jewellery most! This may be due to our colour, which displays jewellery so effectively. In Africa in particular, we have a fantastic range of stunning jewellery from which to choose. There are gold, silver, corals, and glass, stone, metal and pottery beads in all shapes, sizes, textures and colours. These are made up into chokers, pendants, necklaces, waist and hair beads, armlets, anklets and bracelets – jewellery to cover every niche of the body and a few more beside. Then there are crocodile, shark and tiger's teeth combined with gold for necklaces and earrings. Small wonder that we are famous for the superb craftsmanship of our jewellers. Add to these an array of bronze alloy and metal substances, shells like cowries (which once represented money) or large seeds, used sometimes as divining beads, and you begin to get an inkling of the sensational variety of African jewellery.

A big traditional African ceremony is a blaze of colour and reflected light off the precious and semi-precious jewellery and the glinting lurex strands in the local cloth. Such a display is perfect for a really big occasion, but otherwise, don't let the jewellery be too over powering. It is you who should be noticed, not the carats of gold on your body.

STOLES AND SCARVES

Some African fashion incorporates stoles, which can be either draped over the shoulder, or the arm, or wrapped around the body, over the main wrapper. The hand woven ones give a dramatic touch to a simply cut, plain-coloured Western style dress for a party outdoors on a cool evening.

Scarves too are very versatile as accessories. You can wear them on your head, as belts, hat decoration or round your neck. Among the Itsekiris of Nigeria, colourful scarves are held in the hands as part of the traditional dance regalia, and convey messages as they move about in the air, rather like the delicate hand and finger movements of Mali female dancers. For hot climates, light cotton or silk scarves are best, especially when worn as a headtie in the same fabric as your traditional African clothes.

CLOTHES FOR COLDER CLIMATES

It is necessary to mention briefly suitable clothes for warmth in case you live in countries with cold climates or travel to such places regularly, irrespective of the season. While I support fully the concept of promoting our traditional fashion when abroad, some of them are not warm enough. I have seen African women arriving at European airports in the autumn, shivering in their cotton clothes.

Your selection of warm clothes depends on your normal place of residence and frequency of travel. If you visit these countries only once in a while, and usually in the summer, then you will only need about two transitional outfits for cool days. The evenings can be quite chilly too. As you are likely to do some shopping abroad, don't overpack, in order to avoid having to pay excess baggage on the homeward journey (a problem all too common with us.)

COATS

In order to keep warm in colder climates, you will certainly need a coat or jacket, though a good-quality rain coat with a removable woollen lining will serve you very well as an all-year-round coat.

SUITS

Invest in one or two good suits, cut simply so that you can ring the changes with a variety of blouses, choosing lightweight pure wool or gabardine. Our thick traditional woven cloths can be made up lined into elegant and warm suits, but those with large patterns or woven on broad looms should be avoided, as they are difficult to work with.

JUMPERS AND CARDIGANS

Even in Africa, a superb (rather than shapeless) cardigan is useful, draped elegantly over the shoulders in an air-conditioned car, office or restaurant. But in temperate climates, they are invaluable, as temperatures drop with alarming suddeness. Buy this and a comfortable jumper in cashmere, pure wool, shetland or lamb's wool, because these natural fibres are warm, non-itching and will not lose their shape, when carefully washed.

If you enjoy knitting, why not make yourself one or two from the excellent patterns available, or create your own design using small African motifs?

PLANNING THE BASIC WARDROBE

In fashion the colour of our skin is a great asset, because it tones very well with practically all the colours of the spectrum, especially with our brilliant African prints. But the real secret of good fashion sense is knowing when to tone down our love of vibrating patterns and fluorescent hues particularly when in a temperate climate, with little or no sunshine to offset all that brilliance. All very well at night, perhaps, under artificial light, but unless you want to look like a Punk – watch out!

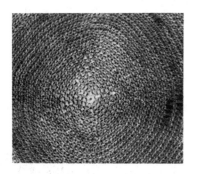

Sometimes it's great to take stock of one's wardrobe, weeding out those clothes one never wears, that don't flatter, and don't go with anything else. To re-plan its contents, try deciding on a basic colour scheme, according to your needs and skin tone. It is more practical to select existing clothes to work around (or the great new purchase), in solid colours, rather than patterned ones. Prints can be difficult to harmonize. Classical colours such as grey, brown, white, black and blue are a good basis on which to start, and have a slenderising effect. Each constitutes an ideal background for the imaginative use of accessories, which can be as bright as you like.

Nigerian indigo tie-dyed cloth, called Al-Kete.

COLOUR

The blaze of colour of African cloth, under the brilliant sun, is a memory to treasure. Various parts of the continent have their colour preferences. In my country, the Ibos love reds and yellows in their George fabrics, while urban Fulanis wear cloths with bold stripes or other large patterns, usually in amber, red or bright saffron shades. Amongst the Ashantis of Ghana, red is used for mourning, while the Yoruba weavers use rich subtle tones like purple and burgundy in stripes.

However one colour that dominates most African fashion is indigo, an earthy colour, deep blue, ageless, timeless like Duke Ellington's 'Mood Indigo.' Wrapped in its range of blues are all the village tones and city rhythms colouring our African life. The blue sky and the sea are reflected on us, flowing from the heads and shoulders of nomads from the Sahara, and the Adire wrappers of our Yoruba grandmothers.

More power to indigo, to the incredible blue depths and beaten shimmering surfaces of an indigo cloth. Yes, my sister, I am writing in praise of indigo, my favourite colour in all its shades of blue. I recommend it highly for all our shades of black. Use it for any kind of casual garment, whether Western or traditional, for the range of patterns and methods of tie-dying give it tremendous possibilities as a fabric. A hat in indigo cloth with a soft droopy brim looks sensational with a white dress. For a cool Harmattan evening or an autumn abroad, wrap yourself in a coat of deep blue indigo cloth, fully lined for warmth.

A coat by Pinky in Aladire fabric.

CHAPTER 9

LEADING A BEAUTIFUL LIFE

'Tread softly, walk with decorum.
An intelligent woman keeps her self-respect
If she falls short of perfect beauty
If her body falls short of perfection.'

This song sung by the East African women hairdressers of Bega, as they work on their intricate hairstyles, reminds their customers about the importance of a woman's behaviour and attitude towards herself, in relation to her beauty – how, in fact, these are reflections of her as an integrated, attractive personality.

In the preceding chapters we have talked about the body, how it works, how to use it, take care of it amd make it beautiful from the inside out. This is only part of the total appeal of a woman, black or white. But the beauty of a well polished personality is also reflected in her behaviour, how she acts and reacts in any situation; how she speaks, walks and interacts with other people. Her charm and warmth will always be obvious, whether in public or in the privacy of her home. These are personal qualities that enhance and complete her beauty, even more than just a lovely face and body.

MANNERS MEAN CONSIDERATION

How often have you heard it said of a stunning woman: 'She may look great, but she is so arrogant.' Lack of courtesy to others – bad manners – will certainly detract from the most perfect face and figure, and make a woman ugly in terms of total beauty. Sometimes a man will choose a woman for her looks, even though all his friends may warn him that she is unsuitable, because of her pride and inappropriate behaviour. But even though love is said to be blind, his eyes will not be clouded forever if she constantly embarasses him in public by her bad manners and her inability to appreciate how she should behave in whatever situation they might find themselves.

We have seen that if we care for our bodies, skin and hair; apply make-up expertly; choose clothes and accessories of quality that suit us; we can radiate an aura of confident and elegant glamour. But an equally important aspect of a beautiful Black woman lies in her human qualities of loving kindness, warmth and courtesy – her consideration for others, whether of a higher or lower status. All these qualities contribute to that most mysterious of inner qualities – charm – perhaps the most difficult of all the human attributes to define and acquire. And yet when we meet someone who has it, who just radiates charm, we sense and respond to it immediately.

CHARM

So what is charm? What kind of people have it? Can anyone acquire it? Can it be learned?

No-one who is bad tempered or consistently bad mannered, has charm. Self-respect, courtesy and a smiling face go hand in hand with charm. People who radiate it, are considerate of others and their feelings. They always try to put people at their ease, especially if they appear uncomfortable in a strange or unfamiliar situation. They are obviously interested in what others have to say and are good listeners. They are never self-centred, but always outward looking. They seem to carry the conviction that their aims in life are right and worth up-holding. From this inner strength they gain self-confidence, courage and peace which, when correctly channelled into wide, deep interests and self-fulfillment, create an intelligent, warm, bright personality – charm, in fact.

So often at a social function the pretty young girls will wonder why men of all ages are clustering around an older woman, well-dressed and elegant perhaps, but certainly no young beauty. So what attracts them? It is obviously her self-confident charm that is so appealing and her obvious interest in others.

Charm is ageless. It is the true expression of your personality, in your looks, smile, warmth, kindness and interest in others and how you relate to them. It is the graciousness that makes other people want to be with you, because they enjoy your company and feel easy and comfortable with you, because you are sincerely interested in them, and are such an interesting person yourself. True charm comes from the soul and a shy person can also be charming in a quiet disarming sort of way. Charm is always sincere. There can be nothing false about it, because when someone is putting on an act, it is only too apparent. Some people are lucky and seem to have been blessed with charm at birth, but its potential is there within us all. We can develop this essential quality, which will bring us friends and make us loved. So how, you may ask, can I do this?

All human beings are unique. We all possess hidden qualities that just need to be brought to the surface and cultivated. Try to concentrate on those special assets you possess and how you can offer them to others in open sincerity. Remember, people will respond to you if you are prepared to go out to meet them half-way, and do not always expect them to come all the way to you with a friendly approach. Their attitude and behaviour towards you will largely reflect your own to them.

A woman who carries herself with grace and dignity and greets others with genuine friendliness and courtesy will be

treated with respect. But on the odd occasion when perhaps her friendliness and sincerity are misunderstood or misinterpreted, she should know how to discourage unwanted advances graciously and firmly.

THE ART OF CONVERSATION

Being able to converse intelligently and easily is an active ingredient of charm. It goes back to your ability to interact with other people. No matter how strikingly beautiful nor how elegantly dressed you are, if you cannot hold an informed conversation or at least listen receptively and with enthusiasm to others, then you are just like a beautiful painting to be admired from a distance, but with no 'life.' Not only do you need to cultivate the ability to listen and respond intelligently, but you should know how and when it is appropriate for you to start a conversation, in either a working or social situation. To be stimulating company, able to talk about a wide variety of subjects and interests, will not only make you more memorable, but enable you to fit in and enjoy yourself anywhere.

This ability to converse freely and easily is much enhanced by a sense of humour, which brings even strangers together, sharing thoughts and ideas in a happy and amusing way. A woman with a sense of humour is a joy. A funny remark will cheer up a dejected crowd waiting in the rain for a bus that may never come. Humour is only in bad taste when it is offensive or directed at the misfortunes of others.

If you are self-conscious and tongue-tied when in the company of those you feel are better educated, more self-confident and more charming than you are, you can do a great deal to help yourself overcome your shyness and reluctance to join in. Try to broaden your mind by reading good local as well as international newspapers, magazines and books. Be knowledgeable about your own culture, and keep up-to-date on your country's politics, business, music, arts and sports. As far as movies, theatre, and television are concerned, we all need to relax sometimes. But an exclusive diet of entertainment films and comedy shows is escapist and belittles your intelligence. Tune in to cultural topics, current affairs and matters affecting your national life generally. This is more fulfilling mentally for you and will enable you to discuss matters in depth and with some authority.

Self-confidence in the art of conversation can be learned and cultivated, but it comes initially from an assured knowledge of people, places, things and important issues of the day, which will enable you to exchange ideas with others, without necessarily agreeing with them. Good background knowledge will help you to sort out your own ideas and form opinions of your own that people will listen to and respect.

FRIENDSHIP

Being in interesting company and enjoying the art of good conversation is the spice of life and one of the main ways in which we make friends. You meet someone and start talking only to find that you have a great many interests in common, similar ideas, likes and dislikes. This can lead to friendship and we all need loyal friends. As the poet John Donne said way back in the 16th century: 'No man is an island entire of itself', and it is just as relevant today. Man is a social animal, and we all need each other. All of us have many acquaintances, but we need, if only a few, real friends for understanding, confidences and help, and to share the fun and laughter, as well as the problems and sorrows. Be truly loyal to your precious female friends, and don't pinch their men!

In many parts of Africa, it is common practice for friends to demonstrate their closeness by dressing similarly, in the same style and materials or colours. In fact it is usual to consult each other about what to wear 'in uniform' to social functions and family gatherings. This may not suit the individualist, who likes to create her own style, but it is a way in which many like to show the world that they are not alone – that they enjoy the solidarity of being part of a close group.

Members of the same Nigerian compound, dressed in matching wrappers, on their way to the Oshun Festival.

YOUR VOICE

An attractive speaking voice is one of the most captivating assets a woman can have. Over-loud and high-pitched voices can be irritating, and shouting, squawking laughter gives a bad impression. Try to cultivate a well modulated, low-pitched voice that is pleasing to the ear; that will reflect your polished personality and enhance your self-confidence, when talking in public either with one person or in a group. Listen to women you admire and note how well they discipline their voices in pitch and tone, depending on where they are and to whom they are speaking.

But the voice is only one part of it. You should speak clearly so that people do not have to strain their ears to listen. It is very irritating to have to keep saying to someone: 'Would you mind repeating that?' If you record your voice on a tape recorder in the privacy of your room, you will be able to hear yourself as others do, and perhaps be able to correct any faults or aspects of your speech with which you are not happy. Speak slowly, pronouncing each word clearly, and don't rush or gabble your words, so that they run into each other. Many people do this when they are nervous. So if you learn to relax in the company of others, your voice will relax too. Imagine how important this is at job interviews, or if your profession or community concerns demand public speaking. Always remember that we communicate not only by the actual words said, but also by the way we say them.

BODY LANGUAGE

Another way in which we sometimes quite unconsciously communicate, is through body language. When we are talking, we make gestures with our hands, our eyes, our facial expressions and movements of the shoulders. Even the way we sit or stand can say a lot about us. So you will want to make all your movements and gestures as controlled and as graceful as possible.

But beware of using body language too provocatively, such as the way you roll your big brown eyes, move your hips as you walk and so on, and in the wrong places at the wrong times, it can create an over-tantalising impression, get you an undeserved bad reputation and could land you in serious trouble!

SOCIAL DECORUM

'Decorum' simply means 'that which is suitable.' In terms of personal conduct and public behaviour, it is a way of enabling people to live together in reasonable harmony. Just as every society has its own concept of physical beauty, so every culture has its ideas of decorum, sometimes called etiquette, as well as moral codes of conduct and sanctions that govern public and private behaviour. Traditional African initiations, age group schools and other forms of social grooming teach attitudes, conduct and the means of fitting into society, often as a preparation for entering the next stage of life, such as puberty or marriage. Heredity and environment also influence human behaviour, but if you feel that yours have not given you all the advantages you need, you can make good many of the deficiencies yourself.

We are all products of the society in which we grew up. If you are not happy with yours – and what society anywhere is perfect? – you should first strive to improve things by your individual contribution within that society. Secondly, concentrate on enhancing and preserving that which is good, and discarding that which is no longer relevant or appropriate to today's world. But don't blindly accept imported ideas and goods, without questioning their value.

Opportunities for education in Western cultures – either overseas or in the educational institutions of the home country sometimes cause Africans to forget or even look down upon their African roots, and regard certain aspects of local culture and morality with disdain. They see educational opportunities away from the home environment as offering all kinds of moral freedom, but they neglect to appreciate that such freedom also carries with it a great deal of social responsibility.

We should never allow long exposure to other cultures to completely change our attitudes to our own, especially those concerning respect for the human dignity of others. The social and moral structures of our societies have grown and developed over the years to hold them together; so that everyone within them knows almost by instinct what is permissable and what is not, if he or she wishes to retain a place of respect within that society.

THE HOME

'The hand that rocks the cradle rules the world'. Though the Black woman of today may be an international executive, she is most probably a homemaker as well, and as such, she has an instrumental role to play. She is the captain of her ship, her home. Family units are the pillars on which any society stands, and the patterns of behaviour and the values of family life have a profound effect on local and national life, as well as on any country's international image. In the home we have a tremendous responsibility for ensuring that our children appreciate good manners as part of personal and social awareness of others.

A harmonious family.

Fathers participating in a children's birthday party.

A well balanced family is one in which both husband and wife share the responsibility for the discipline and behaviour of their children, inside the home as well as out of it. If yours is a one parent family or a polygamous one, in which there may be several children from other wives, a lot more rests on your shoulders. For your children to be well mannered, you and your husband or partner must set good examples for them and teach them to be respectful to people of all kinds. You should never shout at or abuse house servants, especially in front of your children. It is also unpleasant and sometimes frightening for your children to hear you argue or quarrel in front of them. They will lose their sense of security, and also their respect for you both. Your relationship with your partner therefore plays a very important role in the upbringing of your children, and the examples you give them to follow.

PARTNERSHIP

Whether you choose your partner for yourself or whether he is chosen for you in an arranged marriage, two different individuals living together obviously experience problems, especially in respect of irritating, unsuspected bad habits. These have to be lived with or subtly worked on until they are changed, although it is unrealistic to expect radical changes in your partner: 'You can't teach an old dog new tricks.' It is better to let him know in a gentle, humorous way what you find intolerable or offensive in him and ask him to let you know what he finds irritating in you, as neither of you is perfect.

But never nag. Develop a forgiving spirit of compromise and understanding, and once you have forgiven your man, don't reheat his sins for breakfast! Real love between you, the kind that is characterised by kindness, caring, respect for mutual feelings, openness, trust and a sense of humour can make your problems bearable and solvable, and your life together beautiful – when it does work, it is wonderful!

In a polygamous marriage, there are rules governing the relationship between you and your husband and his various wives. These customs are designed to avoid friction and jealousy. Therefore, you must familiarise yourself with these *before* entering into such a marriage and if you agree to them, be prepared to accept them.

No woman can be beautiful, elegant, charming and well-mannered if her home environment is untidy and uncared for, and she herself looks slovenly and unkempt, because she thinks: 'After all, I'm only at home. What do I have to dress up for?' An unloved home is an unhealthy home, so strive to keep your home clean and tidy, and involve your children in maintaining its well being. Your care will reflect the warmth of your love and affection for those who share the home with you, and will greet visitors with an obvious welcome.

Such a home can be an example to others, and in this way you can be a good citizen, making your own contribution to the improvement of your local environment. The women of Kenya have mobilised themselves in a clean-up campaign and a massive tree planting operation to save and beautify their country, not only for today, but for generations to come. Nigeria has formed a National Womens' Environmental Improvement Group to do likewise. Why not encourage your friends to start a local environmental improvement group, if there is not already one established locally? The beauty and cleanliness of your environment is a fine heritage to leave your children.

ENTERTAINING

A party should be a time when your friends can enjoy good company in a relaxed atmosphere.

If you are entertaining, you should have everything ready in advance for your party, whether it is a set dinner party for a few people or a large buffet. So plan well ahead and organize your time so that as much of the food and general arrangements, as well as your own beauty routine and clothes can be attended to in advance. Set out your clothes and accessories the night before.

The main thing to remember about entertaining is that your friends are coming to enjoy good company. You are not entering a party competition, nor are your guests coming to award you medals for the biggest, the most lavish, the best catered party of the year. So if you are relaxed, happy and obviously enjoying your party too, and not looking harrassed or constantly disappearing, then a good time will be had by all. It is being able to create an easy, celebratory, hospitable atmosphere that really counts, with a clever mixture of the right people.

When planning a party and considering the menu, you should make sure that you do not include any foods which may be prohibited to any of your guests. Devout Muslims do not touch pork, and nowadays many people have become vegetarians, some eating no meat, fish or eggs; others just not eating meat, so you should provide some alternatives to meat. Make sure that you have a plentiful supply of soft drinks and fruit juice for those who don't want to drink alcohol, or too much of it.

The seating of your dinner guests at the table is as important as the food, drink and music, so plan beforehand. If there are to be more than six people sitting down, then it is a good idea to have place cards indicating where each guest is to sit. Try to sit a woman and man alternately, but not a husband and wife together. For a small dinner party it is important to get the right mix of people. You want to encourage good conversation during the meal, so avoid loud music which will drown out the sparkling dialogue. Even at a large party, where guests may be dancing later, remember the neighbours, and keep the music down to reasonable levels. Be considerate, like that great black singer Marion Anderson, who never practised her singing when anyone else was near, for fear of disturbing them!

Plan your entertaining well ahead, so that you too can enter the party mood.

TRAVELLING ABROAD

If you have to travel abroad frequently, whether for study, for business, as the wife of a diplomat or just for pleasure as a tourist, it is worth investing in books about the country you are going to and finding out as much as possible – through the embassy or consulate in your capital perhaps – about the country, the people, their culture, customs and behaviour, before you go. Wherever you are travelling the rule must be to observe and respect local customs. 'When in Rome do as the Romans' is a useful maxim.

Check with the embassy or consulate of that country that you get the right type of visa and that you comply with any special health regulations. (Yellow Fever innoculations have to be done ten days before travelling.) Check also what articles are banned (no alcohol is permitted to be taken into many Muslim countries, for instance, nor magazines showing men or women in any stage of undress;) how much money and in what form, you may take with you. An international driving licence is useful for most countries, except those that forbid women drivers.

Never agree to deliver a parcel or letter for anyone unless you are sure of the person and the contents. Terrorists have been known to use unsuspecting girls they meet on holiday to carry parcels or radios which explode in mid-air. If you are found carrying even small amounts of drugs or prohibited amounts of currency, in some countries the penalty is death and in all countries, long imprisonment. The attention of vigilant customs officials tends to focus on those people whose appearance they think is strange or unconventional, or who have excessive baggage. Always travel in simple, comfortable clothes, with neat suitcases and one piece of hand luggage. Don't burden yourself with stuffed carrier bags as hand-luggage, it not only looks inelegant, but it is a nuisance to you and your fellow travellers on a plane.

'What has all this got to do with a health and beauty book for Black women?' you may be saying. My sister, it is all very vital information for you if you travel abroad and especially if it is for the first time. Such information will help you avoid embarrassment, and so enable you to retain your dignity and beauty as a Black woman. Enjoy your travel and don't be too shy, over-cautious or frightened. As a stranger, you will be given a lot of help and forgiven many mistakes. But don't forget that you are an ambassadress for your country and your race. If you behave badly in any way, you are going to make difficulties not only for yourself, but also for others of your countrymen and women.

CLASS

Being Black and beautiful as a whole woman means that you have 'class' – an air of quiet, well mannered elegance and self-assurance – without feeling superior or appearing snobbish in any way. It has nothing to do with wealth or social standing either. Class, like charm, is difficult to define but it is easily and quickly recognisable. It combines all the qualities of self-discipline, and courtesy (good manners and consideration shown to those who serve you just as much as to superiors or those in authority), kindness, charm, warmth, and elegance in appearance. Intelligence, poise and pride in being Black is also part of it.

But this means never forgetting who you are and where you come from and being proud of both. We Black women have a rich heritage in the historically significant lives of our African predecessors, which has been carried to Black America

Statue of Queen Amina of Zaria

and the Caribbean and other Black societies. There can be little doubt that good manners, respect and the significance of 'dignity' deep rooted in our African tribal life, were never wiped out even through slavery or transportation and emigration to foreign lands.

In order to give special recognition and pay homage to some wonderful Black women of the past, whose lives were dedicated to the progress of their societies and of Black women in particular, Johnson Products Company of Chicago, USA, leading manufacturers of cosmetics and hair products for Blacks, sponsored an exhibition in Chicago entitled, 'The Great, Beautiful Black Women', to commemorate the company's Silver Jubilee in 1978. The women in question were selected by a distinguished panel as being outstanding for their beauty, talent, contribution and achievements. All of them had the kind of beauty I have been talking about – complete, wonderful women with brains, ambition and determination to improve, progress and achieve, not only for themselves, but for their Black sisters.

In Africa, women also played (and of course are still playing) outstanding roles as great social reformers and achievers in many fields, in addition to being respected wives and mothers. They recognised that a country in which women lacked opportunities for education and involvement in economic, political and cultural life, was one that would be at a grave disadvantage in relation to its more forward-looking neighbours. Such women as the Nigerians Olufunmilayo Ransome Kuti, Lady Oyinkan Abayomi, Mrs Margaret Ekpo and Queen Amina of Zaria appreciated the difficulties and problems of being pioneers, but they set about the task of improving themselves, changing old repressive attitudes, raising the consciousness of their sisters and thus making their societies better for the women who came after them.

When eventually a few were able to travel abroad for higher education, they never forgot their own culture and traditions. One such example was Sarah Forbes Beneta Davies, also a Nigerian, and believed to be the first African women educated in England. She was a ward of Queen Victoria, but despite this royal connection, she re-adapted herself so well to the indigenous ways of life of her country when she returned, and served her community so splendidly, that her people idolised her.

I salute the many wonderful Black women of the past and the great many today, who combine their traditional roles of wives, mothers, homemakers, agriculturalist and food-providers, with involvement in their communities, and in the health, well being, progress, economic and cultural development of their countries. I share their beauty and achievement with you all, my sisters, by closing this book with a dedication to them.

Women who have achieved international fame

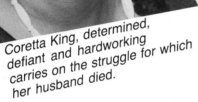

Coretta King, determined, defiant and hardworking carries on the struggle for which her husband died.

Winnie Mandela, internationally famous South African activist.

Miriam Makeba, revolutionary, singer and composer, originally from Azania, now resident in Guinea.

Buchi Emecheta, Nigerian mother of 5 and internationally famous, award-winning novelist.

Successful women artists

Grace Reed, innovative Jamaican fashion-designer and mother.

Nike, mother of 3 and a highly successful Nigerian batik artist.

Houria Niati, Algerian painter achieving international acclaim, yet controversial in North Africa, where women do not normally occupy public positions.

Magdalene Odundo, a Kenyan potter, who exhibits all over the world.

Pam Douglas, a political reformist Jamaican composer, vocalist and mother.

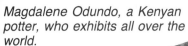

Margaret Busby, successful Ghanaian book-publisher.

Women who have succeeded in the world of business and international affairs

Jewel Lafontant, first Black and first woman to be Deputy U.S. Attorney General.

Eddah Gachukia, educationalist and Member of Parliament who has served Kenya on numerous boards, commissions and organizations

Chief Mrs Opral Benson the traditional chief of fashion in Lagos. She is also a top business woman and Chairman of Johnson Products of Nigeria Ltd.

Lady Ademola, first Nigerian woman to attend Oxford University and a prominent leader and social reformer.

Mrs Hilda Adefarasin, National
President of the National
Council of Women's Societies,
Nigeria.

Francesca Yetunde
Emmanuel, first woman
Permanent Secretary in
the Federal Government
of Nigeria. Permanent
Secretary in the Federal
Ministry of Information,
Social Development
Youth and sport

Dr Sinmi Johnson, first Nigerian
woman Dental Surgeon and
Orthodentist; first Nigerian
woman Vice President of the
Nigerian Olympic Committee;
Chairman of the Women and
Development Committee of the
Federal Government of Nigeria.

Mrs Kuforiji-Olubi,
first woman
Chairman of the
United Bank
for Africa.

SOPHISTICATED PUNK

By Pat Grant-Williams

Hair texture: Medium Fine
Client has received an Ultra Sheen® 2 Conditioning No-Lye Creme Relaxer. It is a new growth service.

1. A. Hair is wet and parted across crown from ear to ear.
B. Establish guideline at right ear by parting from crown part, to temple area horizontally, 1 to 2 inches above the ear. Holding hair at 0° cut horizontally.

2. Repeat step 1A. and 1B. on left side.

3. Establish front guideline by combing hair from crown forward, from eyebrow to eyebrow. Cut at 0°. Connect front guideline to ear at a 45° angle.

4. Begin front layering by establishing guideline in crown area. Part off a section of hair in crown. Hold hair at 180°. Cut hair 3 to 4 inches in crown. This will be used as the guideline for entire front section.

5. Blend or connect top guideline with side(s) by holding hair at 90° angle and cutting vertically. Repeat on opposite side.

6. Part hair down center back from crown to nape area, horizontally 2 to 3 inches above nape. Create weight line by cutting hair at 0° (Same as for bob).

7. Establish 3 or 4 sections in back depending on density of hair by parting hair vertically from crown to nape.

8. Connect back left section to side by holding at 135° and cutting horizontally.

9. Continue blending by bringing all hair up to 135° from nape area in left section to blend with side.

10. Blend initial guideline at crown with back section at 180°. Continue layering back section by connecting previous guideline with the next section holding hair at 135°. Hair should not be longer than 4" to avoid separation.

11. Connect sides to back by over exaggerating forward and cutting at 45°.

12. Finish top by sharking* layers from eyebrow to eyebrow.

*Sharking — using tip of shears strategically to remove hair to aid in support.

Rolling Pattern

Leaflet reproduced by kind permission of Johnson Products Co., Inc.